**The
Leathercraft
Handbook**

An Hachette UK Company
www.hachette.co.uk

First published in the United Kingdom in 2020 by Ilex,
an imprint of
Octopus Publishing Group Ltd,
Carmelite House,
50 Victoria Embankment
London EC4Y 0DZ
www.octopusbooks.co.uk
www.octopusbooksusa.com

Distributed in the US by
Hachette Book Group,
1290 Avenue of the Americas,
4th and 5th Floors
New York, NY 10104

Distributed in Canada by
Canadian Manda Group,
664 Annette St.,
Toronto, Ontario, Canada M6S 2C8

Publisher: Alison Starling
Editorial Director: Zena Alkayat
Commissioning Editor: Zara Anvari
Managing Editor: Rachel Silverlight
Editor: Jenny Dye
Art Director: Ben Gardiner
Designer: Luke Bird
Photography: Hannah Miles
Step-by-step Photography: Mattia Calissano
Assistant Production Manager: Lucy Carter

ISBN 978-1-78157-690-8

A CIP catalogue record for this book is available
from the British Library.

Printed and bound in China

10 9 8 7 6 5 4 3 2 1

The
Leathercraft
Handbook

Candice
Lau

**A step-by-step guide to
techniques and projects**

Contents

Introduction

How I Became a Leather craftswoman

I never set out to be a leather craftswoman.

The whole journey began when I was still a designer working in a digital agency in London back in 2011. My boss offered me an industrial sewing machine one Christmas, and soon after another colleague handed me a leather hide he had sitting around at home. At the time, I was already making fabric bags in my spare time and offering them to friends and family. Eager to create a bag from this piece of leather, I drew straight onto the back and crudely cut into the hide with kitchen scissors. The sewing needle on my machine fumbled its way across the thickness. By the end of the evening, I had made my first leather bag – a beautifully shaped yet terribly stitched piece of work.

I began to seek out workshops, seminars and events across the world to learn the different aspects of leatherwork. My training took me to Hong Kong to learn traditional saddle stitching and back to London where I studied the technical art of pattern making. I then travelled to the Netherlands to understand how to use traditional methods of production to create functional, contemporary designs. Finally I went to Italy to see how the masters work their craft.

Powered by this training, I created my own collection of handcrafted leather bags and accessories. I began to spread my skills by teaching traditional leatherwork to enthusiasts and novices. Sure enough, just as it did for me, these new-found skills led some of them to create their own collections of leather items.

I no longer work in graphic design, yet the skills I learned in my former career have no doubt influenced the bags and accessories I create. Each one of you who is working through this book or has attended one of my classes will have a story of your own, perhaps not dissimilar to mine, of discovering a passion for a craft that sweeps you off your feet. I hope my story and designs throughout these pages will inspire you and become a part of your journey to becoming a leather craftsperson.

How to Use This Book

- - - - - - - - - - - - - - - - - - - -

This book is designed for the novice craftsperson to begin an adventure with leatherwork. We will start off with the materials, tools and essential techniques you'll need. The projects begin with easy makes, and then move on to intermediate and advanced items. We then progress to creating your own designs, by adapting some of the styles and techniques from the earlier projects. You'll learn how you can take the basics from a project and make the design your own.

The best way to begin is to get an overall feel of the book by looking through the essential techniques and then seeing how these are applied in the projects. Use the first four beginner projects to get used to your tools and practise essential techniques, including cutting, pattern making, saddle stitching, strap cutting, burnishing and edge finishing.

Working on the Projects

All the projects in this book, with the exception of the Belt (see p. 76), start with pattern making. A detailed pattern is provided at the beginning of each project and it denotes the exact lengths, widths, prick marks, holes and skive edges that you will need to make. All measurements are given in both metric and imperial. Always use one system or the other; do not mix them.

When cutting the leather, lay out the leather in full, with the grain (finished) side up, across a flat surface with a cutting mat underneath. Always cut on the grain side (unless specified) so that you can see where the best parts of the surface are and arrange the pattern pieces on top. For example, the front pieces of a bag should be placed on the best part of the hide, while the base would benefit from being cut from the centre of the hide where the leather is strongest and least stretchy.

Unless advised otherwise in the instructions, all the leather pieces must be prepared before assembly, which means that holes must be punched, skive edges skived, and notches and prick marks made with the awl. All markings should be made on the grain side unless specified.

For the projects in this book, we will work with a pricking chisel to hammer down the stitch holes in preparation for saddle stitching, rather than a pricking iron which would require you to pierce each mark with an awl to make the holes before stitching. Always use the same size chisel throughout a project unless specified. This is to ensure that when two pieces of leather come together for stitching, the holes will align.

The seam allowances in the projects have been set to 5 mm (¼ in). When instructed to score a stitch line, set the compass to this width. Only a few projects have used a smaller seam allowance, but this is clearly indicated. This also applies to skiving: most skived edges are made 1 cm (⅜ in) from the edge, unless otherwise indicated in the project's instructions.

With this in mind, go forth and enjoy!

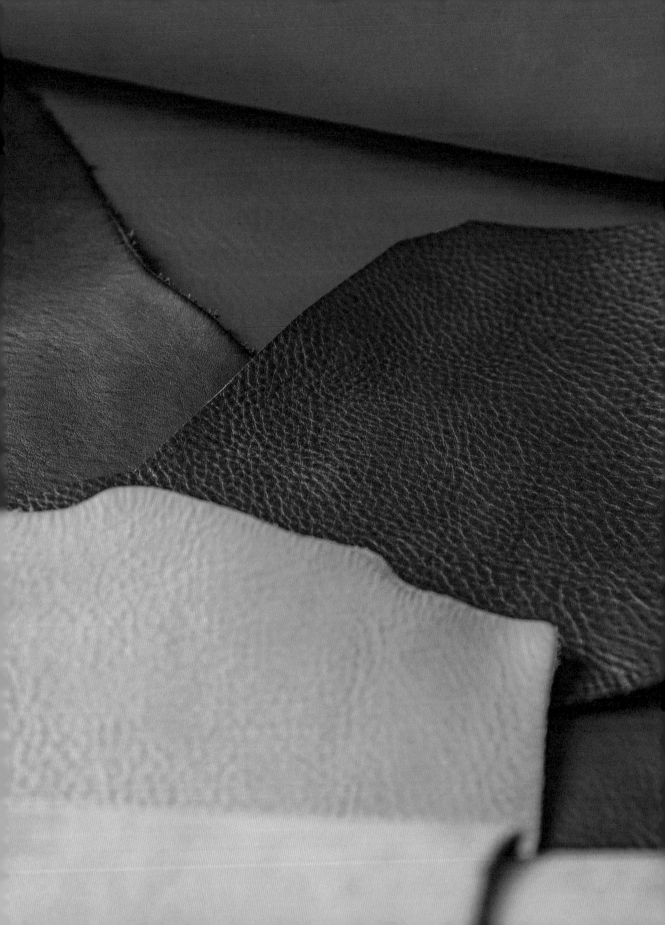

Getting Started

Materials

Leather is one of the oldest and most versatile materials in the world. Humans have used and adapted leather throughout history, from our cave-dwelling ancestors who may have draped a raw hide over a shoulder, to treating it to gain softness and pliability, or making it hard and impenetrable for armour.

Often called "hides" or "skins", leathers are derived directly from the meat industry, so their supply, costs and geography are all dependent on our eating habits. Once the meat is extracted, the skins are salted and shipped to tanneries. There are four stages to tanning: beamhouse, tanning, re-tanning and finishing.

At the beamhouse, the raw hide is soaked in vats or drums of lime to remove the fats and hairs from it. The hide is then stretched out and checked for excess fats that are "fleshed", or scraped off, with a blunt, moon-shaped blade.

The hide is then tanned in a vat of vegetable matter such as tree barks, leaves or mimosa. This method of vegetable tanning is considered one of the most natural ways of tanning. However, over the nineteenth and twentieth centuries, other processes such as chrome tanning have been introduced. Chrome tanning is a more efficient, albeit highly polluting, way of tanning.

You can quite clearly discern the difference between vegetable-tanned and chrome-tanned hides, if not by their look and feel, most surely by their price. Chrome-tanned hides are usually softer and often have minimal surface texture. Vegetable-tanned leathers are considered more beautiful, as they maintain a lot of the natural surface grain and can be burnished to attain a glazed finished edge – hence vegetable-tanned leather commands a higher price.

Oils are then reintroduced into the leather to bring softness. This is done by adding "fat liqueur". The leather is then re-tanned, where dyes or pigments are added or surface textures embossed. The leather is stretched out to dry, uneven thicknesses are shaved off to achieve uniformity, and rough edges are removed.

In the finishing stage, a top coating is sprayed on to fix dyes. Coatings can make the leather glossy or matte, or special effects can be used – for example, to achieve an antique, worn look – before the leather is sent off to the leather merchant.

Different Types of Leather and Their Uses

If you are just starting off with leatherwork, the best way to decide on the right type of leather for your project is to get to know the terminology and where the different types of leather come from.

Basic Terminology

Hide
Refers to leather from larger animals, usually bovine, which includes cows and buffaloes. These are the most common hides and are often used for bags, accessories and furnishings.

Skins
These are leathers from smaller animals such as sheep and goats. Skins are most often used for clothing, as they tend to be soft and pliable.

Exotics
These command a very high price and come from animals such as crocodiles, alligators, ostriches and pythons. Most of these fall under the endangered list of almost 6,000 species that are protected by the Convention on International Trade in Endangered Species (CITES). Skins purchased under this convention must be issued with a CITES certificate to prove that they follow its process from capture to the end consumer. Heavy fines are imposed if found without the certificate and the items will be confiscated.

Butt, shoulder and belly
A piece of leather is normally divided into these three parts. The butt is the strongest part, with tight fibres. The shoulder has more uneven and loose fibres and is recognizable by the stretch marks created by the animal moving its head. The most fibrous and stretchy part is the belly.

Grain side
This refers to the finished top side of the leather.

Splits
These are leathers that have been cut horizontally from the hide. They are the corium layers of the hide (see p. 14), where the fibres are more loose and uneven but can be engineered to create more density. These types of leathers are the cheaper range in the market. This term also describes the action of thinning down the hide. Small pieces can be hand split, and bigger pieces are often split on large machines with a sharp horizontal blade.

Types of Hide

- - - - - - - - - - - -

Bovine hides are the main type of leather we will use for the projects. The thickness of the hide is approximately 5 cm (2 in) and from this thickness it is split to create different types of leather.

Cross-Section of a Hide

- - - - - - - - - - - - - - - - - - - -

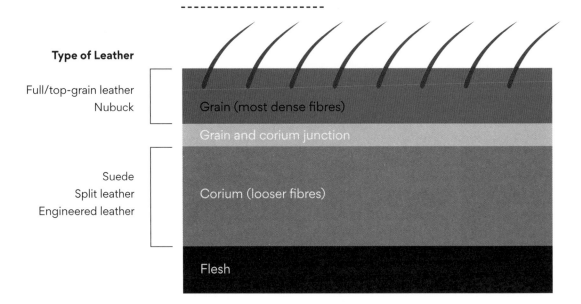

Type of Leather

Full/top-grain leather
Nubuck

Suede
Split leather
Engineered leather

Grain
In this section you would find leathers such as nubuck, napa, top grain or oily pull-up. These leathers are split from the top of the hide and the fibres are dense and strong. Top grain, oily pull-ups and napa are finished on the top side, while nubuck is further sanded down on the grain side to create its velvety feel. A full grain hide is a piece of leather that contains the entirety of the top-grain section. These types of leather are best used for bags, accessories, shoes and some upholstery.

Corium
The fibres of the corium layer are much more sparse. Suede is split on large machines with a horizontal blade and then sanded down on the flesh side. Suede is normally used for linings of bags or clothing, as it is not as hard wearing as grain hides. The remaining parts of the corium layers are shaved down to create artificial, engineered leather or PU split, finished with a coating of laminate or pigments. These will not wear over time like grain hide and will maintain the laminate appearance. These types of leather are considered of lesser value and are great for initial prototyping.

Tools

- - - - - - - -

While the most costly aspect of leathercraft is the leather itself, it is not too expensive to set up for your first project. A beginner's set of eight tools will cost no more than an entry-level sewing machine would, and a knife, cutting mat, metal ruler, awl, pricking chisel, hammer, harness needles and waxed thread will be sufficient to get you started. With most of these fitting into a pencil case, you can work on a kitchen table, a desk, on wooden floors, or even travel with them as I have done. Essentially, this is how I started. However, as I got more into leatherwork, my toolkit began to grow and I now have a studio full of equipment.

There is a vast selection of tools that you can invest in, and it can become rather overwhelming with so many tools that seemingly do the same thing. As you master the craft, you'll get to know their different uses. For now, what I have included in the lists below would be sufficient for someone working through all the projects in this book.

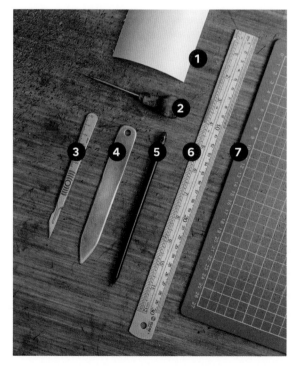

For pattern making you will need:

1. **Pattern paper** or **250 gsm manilla card** (100 lb cardstock)
2. **Awl** – a small pointed tool used to scratch, mark or make holes.
3. **Utility knife** or scalpel.
4. **Bone folder** – a dull-edged tool that helps to make creases or folds.
5. **Sharp pencil**
6. **Metal ruler**
7. **Cutting mat**

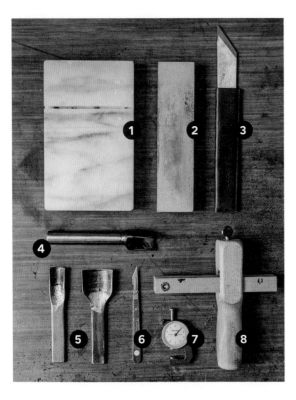

For cutting you will need:

1. **Granite/marble block** – a smooth surface used when skiving.
2. **Sharpening stone** – used to sharpen the paring knife.
3. **Paring knife** – designed specifically to remove thickness from edges of leather.
4. **Strap end punches** – round, dome- or triangular-shaped tools used to efficiently hammer out these shapes at the ends of straps.
5. **Corner punches** – curved tools that allow you to punch out fixed-shape rounded corners.
6. **Clicking knife** or scalpel– with removable blades that can be replaced when blunt.
7. **Thickness gauge** – used to measure the thickness of leather.
8. **Strap cutter** – a wooden instrument with adjustable widths that enables you to cut straps by aligning it against a straight cut edge.

For punching holes and setting rivets you will need:

1. **Hammering block** – a pad to hammer on that absorbs sound and vibration.
2. **Crew punches** – oval-shaped hole punches often used to cut slots for buckles.
3. **Wooden/rawhide mallet** – a hammering tool with a wooden or rawhide head that absorbs sound and vibration when hit against metal hole punches and chisels.
4. **Hole punch set** – the varying sizes enable you to punch holes through paper and leather.
5. **Rivet setter** – a toolset that comprises a metal base with varying sizes of rounded grooves and a setter. It is used to tighten rivets.
6. **Pippin punch** – used to create keyholes for Sam Browne stud fastenings.

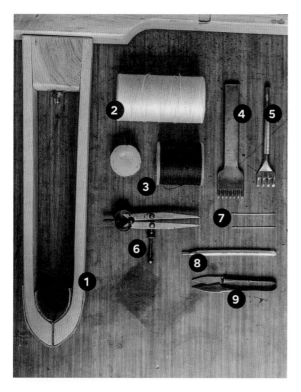

For pricking and stitching you will need:

1. **Stitch pony or stitching clamp** – a wooden clamp to hold the leather in place while stitching.
2. **Ready-waxed polyester threads**
3. **Linen thread and beeswax** – linen threads must be waxed with beeswax before use.
4. **Pricking chisel** – allows you to punch straight through the leather, for a much easier stitching process. The sizing is normally denoted by the stitch length.
5. **Pricking iron** – after hammering the pricking iron down lightly to create the marks, an awl is used to turn each mark into a hole prior to stitching.
6. **Divider** – a compass with two pointed ends. Used to score stitch lines before stitch holes are made.
7. **Harness needles** – blunt needles for stitching leather.
8. **Silver pen** – a pen with silver ink that rubs off leather. It is best to test on small scraps first.
9. **Scissors** – for cutting thread.

For finishing you will need:

1. **Gum tragacanth** – a type of resin used for burnishing leather edges to create a smooth, glazed finish.
2. **Sandpaper** (600–1000 grit) – used to remove loose fibres and create smooth edges.
3. **Awl** – to apply edge paint.
4. **Leather-palm glove** – a thick suede glove used to burnish strap edges efficiently.
5. **Polish** – such as mink oil paste, leathercare – used to polish the grain side of leather.
6. **Small brush** – to apply gum tragacanth.
7. **Edge paint** – such as acrylic dyes.
8. **Cotton cloth** – this can be used as a replacement for the burnisher.
9. **Beveller** – a tool with a small blade that takes off a sliver of leather from edges to create a rounded edge.
10. **Burnisher** – a rounded wooden tool used to rub leather edges to burnish them.

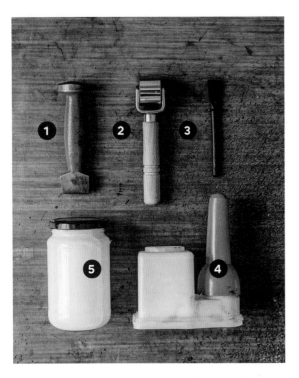

For sticking leather pieces together you will need:

1. **Palm hammer** (with a rounded top) – used to hammer down folds.
2. **Roller** – a heavy metal roller with a wooden handle to make creases, roll seams open or press down glued pieces.
3. **Plastic paddle** – for applying glue. A brush can be used as a replacement for the plastic paddle.
4. **Neoprene glue** – a highly toxic adhesive. If you use this, make sure you're in a well-ventilated space and wear latex gloves.
5. **Water-based or latex glue** – a less toxic adhesive than neoprene glue.

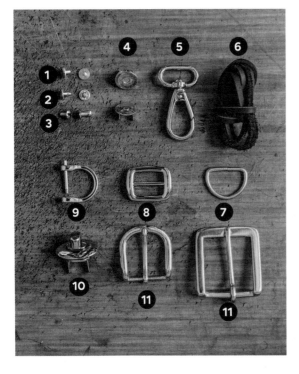

You will also need some basic hardware:

1. **Screw-in rivet** – has a rounded cap and is attached by screwing the top piece to the stem.
2. **Rivet** – a rounded cap fastener.
3. **Sam Browne stud** – a type of closure in the shape of a bulb that comes in various sizes.
4. **Magnets**
5. **Swivel hook** – a hook that is often used for the ends of straps to enable you to detach the straps from the D-ring on the bag.
6. **Leather cord**
7. **D-ring** – often used to attach straps to a bag.
8. **Slider** – a rectagular or oval-shaped piece of hardware with a bar in the centre. Used for adjustable straps.
9. **D-ring** with detachable bar.
10. **Turn lock** – a type of closure.
11. **Buckle** – an adjustable fastening often used for belts.

Workshop

- - - - - - - - - - - - - - -

There are a few basic guidelines that will make your space more work friendly, and hopefully save you from backache.

If your space allows, a bench top measuring a minimum of 1.5 × 1.5 m (5 × 5 ft) at waist height with a 5-mm (¼-in) thick cutting board on top is best. Most vegetable-tanned hides come in a quarter size that will sit nicely on top of the table. Most of the cutting and hole punch work will be done standing up as you will achieve better accuracy when you hover over the work, so waist height is ideal.

To prevent creasing, all leather should be rolled and never folded for storage. A great place to put your material is under the table, away from sunlight to prevent discolouration. Always roll leather on the grain side and place light and dark colours separately, as darker colours can smudge onto lighter ones, especially on naturally tanned hides.

Tools should be separated based on their function and to allow easy access. Dyes and adhesives should also be placed away from sunlight to preserve their quality.

Essential Techniques

There are several essential techniques that are applied to most projects, and these include pattern making, cutting, gluing, saddle stitching, edge finishing and attaching hardware. This section is not only about perfecting the techniques to create refined finishes, but also about handling the tools for these basic skills.

Pattern Making

It can be tempting to cut straight into the leather and see your project take shape immediately. However, making a mistake on an expensive material within the first hour of your work can be disheartening. For this reason it is imperative that you start off by creating a pattern.

Personally, I find pattern making one of the most interesting aspects of the process. Working out the mathematics of the construction is really the first part of seeing your project come to fruition. With your pattern pieces cut precisely, you can use tape or staples to join the pieces together and create a card prototype. Any mistakes and changes can be revised on your pattern before you move on to the leather.

You will need to draw the patterns onto pattern card, using the following methods for accurate shapes. In this section I will demonstrate the basic rules for pattern making, which can then be applied to all shapes and sizes of patterns in the projects throughout the book.

Cutting a rectangle

For this example, we will make a rectangular pattern piece measuring 26 × 18 cm (10¼ × 7 in).

You will need:
Pattern card or 250 gsm manilla card
      (100 lb cardstock), at least A4 (letter) size
Cutting mat
Bone folder
Sharp pencil or marker pen
Awl
Metal ruler
Utility knife or scalpel

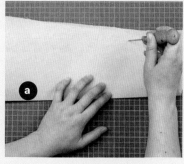

1. For every pattern, begin by creating a straight edge with a perpendicular fold line. Take a piece of card larger than the dimensions of the pattern. Fold it in half and press the folded edge down with the bone folder. It doesn't matter at this stage if the sides are not straight or do not meet. This process shows you how to create a perfect rectangle. Label this fold edge the "first fold".

2. With the folded edge at the base, make a prick mark with your awl on the top right corner, deep enough to go through both layers of the card.

a. First fold

3. Open up the card, place the ruler from prick mark to prick mark and cut along it with the utility knife. You have now created a right angle with the newly cut edge and fold line.

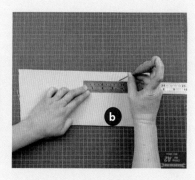

4. Refold your card at the first fold. Lay the ruler parallel to the folded edge and measure 26 cm (10¼ in) from the cut edge. Make a prick mark with the awl, again piercing through both layers of the card. Open the card out again, lay your ruler from mark to mark and cut along it. You have now created two parallel cut edges, 26 cm (10¼ in) apart.

5. Fold the card by aligning the two cut edges, making sure they are perfectly flush with each other before pressing down the fold with the bone folder. You now have two folds that cross in the centre of the pattern. Label the second fold.

6. Place the end of the ruler (at 0 cm/ 0 in) at the first fold line, measure half of 18 cm (7 in) – so 9 cm (3½ in) – and make a prick mark.

b. Second fold

7. Open up the pattern once more and fold your card up at the first fold. You will see the two prick marks that you've just made. Place your ruler from mark to mark and cut along it, through the two layers of card.

8. Open your pattern out in full and you will find that you have created a perfect rectangle of 26 × 18 cm (10¼ × 7 in), with all your corners as right angles. Mark the corners as right angles.

Cutting non-standard shapes

Some patterns will require you to create shapes such as tapered sides or rounded corners. For this example, I will create a shape with both of these features.

14 cm (5½ in)

12 cm (4¾ in)

10 cm (4 in)

1. Measure out the pattern in the largest dimension as a rectangle. In this case, cut a rectangle 14 × 12 cm (5½ × 4¾ in) by following the method in "Cutting a rectangle" on pages 20–2.

2. Fold the pattern again on the vertical first fold. Place the ruler down at the bottom edge, measure 2 cm (¾ in) in from the cut side and make a prick mark with the awl. Note that we are taking off 2 cm (¾ in) from each side because the pattern is folded, thus reducing the bottom width by 4 cm (1½ in) to attain the correct width of 10 cm (4 in).

3. Place the ruler from the top right corner to the prick mark and cut off this triangular shape with your utility knife.

4. With the pattern still folded, draw in the rounded corner with a pencil. Then use your knife to cut this off.

Follow the same technique for cutting rounded corners on leather as shown on page 24. Unfold the pattern once you've completed the cut and you will have the desired pattern shape.

Cutting Leather

Cutting with a knife

You will need:

Clicking knife or scalpel
Small pliers
Cutting mat
Metal ruler

1. To achieve a clean cut, make sure your knife is sharp. If it is not, change the blade using pliers.

2. Lay your leather flat on top of the cutting mat, grain side up. Hold the clicking knife with your index finger on top of the knife at about 45 degrees to the shaft, and your little finger resting on the flat surface. Angle the blade at 45 degrees to the leather. Place the metal ruler against the edge of the pattern and the knife against this edge.

3. Press the knife down and into the leather at the top of the cut. With pressure, drag the knife down towards you, keeping the blade against the edge of the ruler.

4. If the cut hasn't gone completely through the leather, slot your knife back into the cut line and cut again, following the first incision.

Cutting rounded corners

You will need:

Cutting mat
Awl
Clicking knife or scalpel

1. It is best to have your straight edges cut already before moving on to your curves. Position the leather with the pattern on top on the cutting mat near the corner of your work table, so that you can move around the leather (rather than moving the leather around).

2. Score the curved edge with an awl by tracing the pattern. Then remove the pattern piece.

3. Press the blade down into the leather at the beginning of the curve. With pressure, drag the knife around your scored line. Keep the leather in place with the pressure of your hand on top and close to the cut edge while you move around the leather. If the cut hasn't gone completely through the leather, slot your knife back in at the top of the curve and follow the curve again until the cut is complete.

Cutting small rounded corners

- - - - - - - - - - - - - - - -

You will need:

Cutting mat

Clicking knife or scalpel

1. Place the top of the blade at the beginning of the scored curve and angle it at about 5 degrees to the top straight edge. Then make a straight cut to take off the first bit of your curve.

2. Place your knife back on the edge of the leather where your cut edge meets the scored curve, angle it another 5 degrees away from the last straight cut, and trim away another small piece of leather.

3. Continue making small straight cuts, each angled about 5 degrees from the last, until your curve is cut.

Cutting a strap/belt

- - - - - - - - - - - - - - - -

You will need:

Clicking knife or scalpel

Cutting mat

Metal ruler

Strap cutter

1. Using a sharp clicking knife and your metal ruler to guide you, cut a straight line down the edge of the leather on a cutting mat.

2. Adjust the strap cutter to the desired width of your strap or belt.

3. Bring the strap cutter to the top of the leather and align the flat wooden edge to the straight edge you've just cut. Keeping the flat wooden edge against your cut edge, drag the strap cutter all the way down to the desired length of your strap or belt. Use the knife, metal ruler and cutting mat to cut across the width of the strap or belt at the desired length.

Skiving

- - - - - - -

Skiving or paring is used to reduce the thickness on the edges of leather. The aim is to begin at the original thickness of the hide and slide the knife at an angle towards the edge, cutting off some of the leather, creating a diagonal slope.

You will need:
Sharpening stone
Paring knife
Granite/marble block

1. Sharpen the paring knife. Depending on which type of sharpening stone you are using, wet or oil the surface before sharpening. Hold your knife tightly with one hand and press the blade flat on the stone by pressing your fingers on top of it. Push the blade up (away from you) with pressure, then bring it back down and repeat this action.

2. Place the leather grain side down on the granite or marble block, as the knife will need to glide off the leather onto this surface. Do not do this on a cutting mat, as the knife won't glide off but will cut into the mat and become blunt. Hold your knife at the angle you wish to skive off. This is usually 10 degrees to the edge you are skiving. Beginning on the right-hand side, glide your blade from right to left until the edge is skived off. Reverse this from left to right if you are left handed.

Hammering holes, strap ends and corner punches

- - - - - - - - - - - - - - - - - - -

At this stage, you may not have invested in tools such as strap end and corner punches as these can also be cut with a clicking knife. However, the technique for using these types of punches is the same as for punching holes.

You will need:
Hammering block
Hole punch set
Mallet

1. Place the leather on the hammering block. Place the hole punch on top of the leather, perpendicular to the table.

2. Making sure the hole punch is absolutely vertical, hammer down with force with the mallet.

Transferring the Pattern

You will need:

Pattern

Hole punch set

Hammering block

Mallet

Awl

Silver pen

Roller or palm hammer

There are several markings you'll need to make on the project patterns, including stitch lines, rivet and magnet positions, holes and fold lines. You will always need to refer to the pattern, as you won't be able to include all these details on the leather itself. The steps below show you how to transfer the key markings to your leather.

1. Ensure that all the relevant prick marks, stitch lines, folds and holes are marked on your card pattern. Use the correct size hole punches to make the holes in the pattern. Place the pattern on the grain side and cut your leather piece. You can place a heavy object on top of the pattern to prevent it from moving as you cut, or trace around the pattern with an awl before removing the pattern and cutting into the leather.

2. Prick marks: place the pattern over the cut leather piece. Markings such as prick marks for the beginning and end of a stitch line, and the position of studs, rivets, magnets or other closures, should always be made on the grain side using an awl unless otherwise specified. Push the awl through the mark on the pattern and into the leather, but do not let the awl go all the way through the leather. These marks only need to be visible for you.

3. Holes for rivets, magnets, studs and other rounded hardware: make a prick mark at the centre of the hole so that, when you place the hole punch over this mark, the radius is even all around it. Hammer the hole using the mallet and correct size of hole punch immediately after making each prick mark to avoid confusion later on. You can remove the pattern before punching the hole or keep it on the leather as shown above.

4. Folds: to transfer folds, mark a notch at each end of the fold with a silver pen.

Make the fold by pressing it down with your hand first and then making the crease using a roller or palm hammer.

Gluing

Glue is often applied to two leather pieces before they are stitched together, to ensure the pieces stay in place. It is also used to join two pieces before they are burnished to create a smooth edge (see p. 33).

(see p. 33).

You will need:
Leather glue
Plastic paddle or brush
Roller or palm hammer

1. Glue must be applied to a rough surface for it to bond effectively. If gluing on the grain side, scratch the surface with an awl before applying the glue. Using a small plastic paddle or brush, apply a thin layer of glue to both pieces of the leather you wish to glue together.

2. Wait for about a minute for the glue to become tacky and then press the two sides together.

3. Roll over the glued pieces with a roller to press the pieces together. If you don't have a roller, use a rounded palm hammer to hammer down gently.

Saddle Stitching

Saddle stitching is the traditional method of hand stitching for leather. It differs from normal stitching as it uses two needles to weave the thread down previously made stitch holes. Pricking chisels come in a variety of sizes – make sure you use the same chisel throughout a project (unless instructed otherwise) so that the holes will align.

You will need:

Divider
Hammering block
Pricking chisel (any size)
Mallet
Scissors
Waxed thread
2 harness needles
Stitch pony (optional)

1. Set your divider to the desired seam allowance width.

2. Place one point of the divider off the edge of the leather and the other on the leather. Score a line by dragging the divider along the edge of the leather. This method ensures equal distance from the edge of the leather throughout. If you are scoring a stitch line in the middle of the piece, use a metal ruler and align it from prick mark to prick mark before scoring a line using an awl.

3. Place your pricking chisel along the score line. Unless you are starting at a prick mark, place the first prong off the edge of the leather, so that when you apply the same method on the adjoining piece of leather, your stitch holes will match up. Hammer down with force with your mallet two or three times. Lift up the leather to see whether light shines through all the holes. If it doesn't, hammer once again with the pricking chisel or use your awl to push through the holes individually.

4. Place the first prong of the chisel on the last hole you made and, following the score line, hammer down. Repeat this process until you reach the end of the score line. It is good practice to always hammer towards yourself, as this allows you to see the score line for a more accurate placement of the chisel.

5. Repeat steps 1–4 for the adjoining piece of leather.

6. Measure the amount of thread you will need by cutting 4–5 times the length of the line you are going to stitch.

 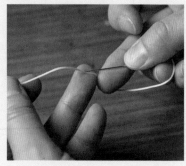 

7. Pull approximately 10 cm (4 in) of thread through the eye of the first needle.

8. Push the tip of the needle into the centre of the thread about 4 cm (1½ in) down from the end of the thread that you have just pulled through the eye.

9. Pull the needle through the thread to create a tight, flat knot.

10. Repeat steps 7–9 on the other end of the thread with the second needle. You now have a piece of thread with a needle on each end.

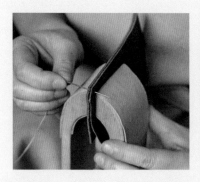 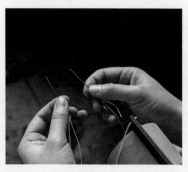 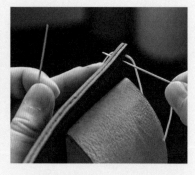

11. Glue the pieces together (see p. 28) before stitching to create a neat, flush edge. To clamp your pieces on the stitch pony, pull the clamp open with one hand and slot the leather in with the other. Release the clamp, allowing the wooden jaws to come back together. Using the stitch pony is optional – you can simply hold your pieces.

12. Push one needle from right to left through the first hole and pull through.

13. Hold both needles up and ensure that you have an equal amount of thread on both sides.

14. Now push the right needle into the second hole and pull through to the other side, so that it becomes the second needle on the left.

15. Take the first needle on the left and push it through the second hole, where the other needle has just come out.

Avoid crossing the threads by holding the thread already in the hole tight to one side before pulling the first needle on the left through the same hole.

16. Pull both threads at the same time on either side to tighten the stitch before you continue this process all the way down the seam, inserting one needle from right to left, then the other needle from left to right through the same hole.

 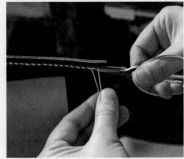

17. Once you have reached the end, back stitch two stitches using the same method.

18. Back stitch one more stitch with just one of the needles, so that both threads are on the same side (usually the side that is less likely to be seen). Cut off the threads at the tip using your scissors. Alternatively, push the needle partially into the next hole and angle it so that you can push it through into the seam and cut the thread on the edge, between the two pieces. Do the same with the other needle. You have now created your first line of saddle stitching.

Tacking

This is a form of hand stitching where you loop the thread three to four times through one hole and over the edge, or through two holes. It is a way of reinforcing weaker areas such as the top of a strap.

You will need:

Awl or 1-mm hole punch
Hammering block (optional)
Mallet (optional)
Scissors
Waxed thread
Harness needle

1. Align the two pieces of leather that will be tacked together. In the position where you want the stitch, push the awl through to create holes through both pieces, or punch a hole no larger than 1 mm in diameter (see page 26).

2. Thread the needle with a 25-cm (10-in) length of waxed thread. Pull the needle from the back side through the front hole only, holding about 5 cm (2 in) of thread at the back. Bring the needle over the edge and secure the thread with a double knot at the back.

3. After ensuring the knot is tight, cut off the end leaving a 2-mm (1/16-in) tail.

4. Bring the needle over the edge again and this time push the needle through the front hole from the grain side, through the hole on the back piece of leather. Loop the thread over the edge and push the needle through both holes again. Do this 2–3 times.

5. Bring the needle to the front; this time, push through the front hole and between the two layers of leather. You might need to pull the seam open to do this.

6. Push the needle through the bunch of threads in between the layers and pull until you see a loop of thread. Put the needle through this loop and pull tight to create a knot. Repeat once.

7. Bring the scissors in between the layers of leather and cut off the thread, leaving a 2-mm (1/16-in) tail.

Edge Finishing

Edge finishing is a way of creating a more refined finish. Bevelling and burnishing only work on vegetable-tanned leather. To achieve a beautiful finish, it is best to use a leather with a thickness of at least 1.8 mm (4½ oz). However, you can apply edge paint to any type of leather.

Bevelling

Bevelling creates roundness on a cut edge.

You will need:
Beveller
Sandpaper (600–1000 grit)

Burnishing

Once you have bevelled your edges, you can burnish the edge to create a smooth, glazed finish.

You will need:
Gum tragacanth (or you can use water or even saliva!)
Small brush
Burnisher (or a cotton cloth)

1. Place the leather on a flat surface with the grain side facing up. On the cut edge, set your beveller at 45 degrees at a point closest to you.

2. Keep this 45 degree angle and push the beveller up along the edge of the leather. You will see a sliver of leather come off to reveal a beautifully rounded edge.

3. Smooth out the edges further by sanding them down with a 600–1000 grit sandpaper.

1. Apply a thin layer of gum tragacanth (derived from tree sap) with a brush. This soaks into the leather to create the smooth surface. Work on approximately 5 cm (2 in) at a time.

2. Take the burnisher or cloth and rub the edge vigorously to create a smooth surface. The smooth and shiny edge that is created is similar to the effect created by rubbing moisturizer on our skin.

Burnishing straps

This is a slightly different method that you can use to burnish straps efficiently.

You will need:
Gum tragacanth (or you can use water or even saliva!)
Small brush
Leather-palm glove

1. Prepare your straps by bevelling (see p. 33) the edges. Then apply a thin layer of gum tragacanth to both edges of the entire strap.

2. Using a leather-palm glove, hold the edge of the strap between your thumb and index finger at the purlicue. Keep the gloved hand in place, and grab the end of the strap with the other hand and pull the strap down. This action burnishes the edges. Repeat this process 4–5 times to achieve a smooth, burnished edge.

Edge painting

This technique is a way of adding a touch of colour to your project.

You will need:
Awl
Edge paint
Sandpaper (600–1000 grit)

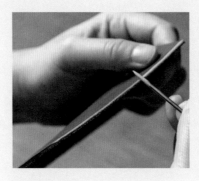 

1. Prepare the edge of your leather by bevelling (see p. 33) and sanding down to create a smooth edge. Dip about 1 cm (⅜ in) of the awl tip into the edge paint.

2. Starting at one end, glide the paint onto the edge of the leather towards you about 2 cm (¾ in) at a time. You want to create a thick layer of paint on the edge. Dip the awl back into the paint and bring it back to the edge to continue painting.

3. Wait for the paint to dry completely. You may decide to apply a second, third or fourth coat. If so, sand down the edge with light pressure using fine sandpaper before the next application. This will get rid of any lumps created in the first application and allow the wet paint to adhere to the surface.

Attaching Hardware/ Accessories

Accessories or hardware are used in leatherwork to embellish or, more importantly, to attach additional elements such as straps. There are several essential hardware attachments in the projects: rivets, Sam Browne studs and magnets.

Setting rivets

Most bags and accessories make use of rivets to join pieces of leather. It can be an efficient method of joining pieces in place of hand stitching. Rivets come in various types and sizes. The sizes of rivets are identified by the size of the cap and the stem length. The stem length should always be a tiny amount (around 1 mm) longer than the thickness of your leather. If it is too long, it will bend when hammered down; if it is too short, it runs the risk of not meeting the cap and thus not holding the two pieces of leather together.

Setting a standard rivet

A standard rivet consists of two pieces: the cap and the stem. When hammered down with the rivet setter, it presses the leather tight in between these two pieces. The rivet setter includes a base with varying groove sizes, which allows you to set different size caps, and a setter, which is a metal stem with a groove on one end to place over the cap. The grooves maintain the dome shape of the rivet. If you would prefer to have a flat surface, you can hammer straight down onto the rivet.

You will need:

Hammering block

Hole punch (same size as rivet)

Mallet

Rivet

Rivet setter

1. For this example we will attach two pieces of leather together. Punch a hole through each piece of leather with the hole punch and mallet. Align the two holes and put the stem part of the rivet through the holes from back to front.

2. Place the cap over the tip of the stem to sandwich the leather in between.

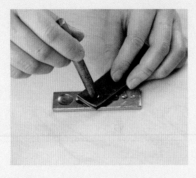 

3. Place the bottom of the rivet on the rivet setter base and the setter on top of the rivet.

4. Make sure the setter is absolutely vertical before hammering down with force to set the rivet in place.

Setting a screw-on rivet

A screw-on rivet includes one piece with a cap and stem, and also a screw thread. It has a set stem length so if the leather is slightly thicker, it will press down tight. If the leather is thinner than the stem length, it can swivel around the stem loosely.

You will need:

Hammering block
Hole punch (same size as rivet stem)
Mallet
Screw-on rivet
Superglue
Screwdriver to fit the screw-on rivet

1. Punch a hole through the leather. Insert the screw thread through the hole from the back. Add a small drop of superglue to the top of the screw thread.

2. Twist on the cap loosely so that it is set in place. Turn the piece on its side, so that you can see the back. Take the screwdriver and, while holding on to the cap, screw the rivet tight from the back to secure it.

Attaching a Sam Browne stud

The Sam Browne stud is an ideal closure. It is made up of a bulb with a stem, which comes in varying sizes, and the adjoining piece: the screw thread. When selecting your Sam Browne stud, take note of the bulb size, stem length and the screw thread length – which should be longer than the thickness of the leather that you are using.

You will need:

Hammering block
3-mm (⅛-in) hole punch
Mallet
Sam Browne stud
    (medium-size bulb)
Superglue
Clicking knife or scalpel
Cutting mat

1. On one piece of the leather, punch a 3-mm (⅛-in) hole. Push the screw thread of the Sam Browne stud from the back to the grain side and apply a drop of superglue to the tip of the screw thread.

2. Twist the bulb and stem on, sandwiching the leather in between.

3. On the second piece of leather, create the keyhole that goes over the bulb of the Sam Browne to form the closure. Punch a 3-mm (⅛-in) hole through the leather. Carefully place the tip of the knife blade 5 mm (¼ in) above the hole. Position the blade so that it comes towards the very centre of the hole. Push the knife blade into the leather to create an incision. You can also use a pippin hole punch to make this keyhole shape, although this tool is often costly.

Attaching a snap closure magnet

Snap closure magnets consist of two pieces (male and female) and are secured to the leather with extended prongs at the back.

You will need:

Snap magnet
    (male and female sides)
Clicking knife
Mallet
Awl
Leather glue
Plastic paddle or brush

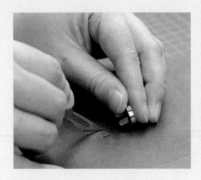 

1. Place the magnet over the prick mark (see p. 27) so that the two prongs are evenly spaced either side of this mark. Push down a little so that the prongs mark the leather. Using a sharp knife, make two incisions where the marks from the prongs are. Slot the prongs of the magnet through these two incisions from the grain side, so that the prongs appear on the back.

2. Turn the leather over, fold the prongs down towards each other and hammer them down so they are flat.

3. To cover the back of the magnet, cut a small piece of leather, place it on top of the back of the magnet and score around it with an awl. Remove it before applying a thin layer of leather glue within the score line. Also apply a thin layer of glue to the back of the small piece of leather.

4. Once the glue has dried a little so that it is tacky, stick the leather piece down. Repeat this process with the corresponding magnet piece.

Attaching a
flat magnet

- - - - - - - - - - -

These magnets are flat discs that are
available in many different sizes and
attached using strong glue.

You will need:

2 flat disc magnets (any size)

Superglue

Awl

Leather glue

Plastic paddle or brush

1. Apply superglue to one side of the
magnet and glue it down in position
on the back of the leather, centring
the magnet over the prick mark on
the leather. While you wait for the
glue to dry, cut a small piece of leather
approximately 1 cm (⅜ in) wider than
the diameter of the magnet.

2. Place the leather piece over the
magnet and score around it using
an awl. Apply leather glue within
the scoreline and on the back
of the small piece of leather.

3. Once tacky, glue the small piece of
leather down over the magnet. Repeat
this process for the corresponding
magnet, but make sure you test which
side attracts the magnet already in
place before you glue it down.

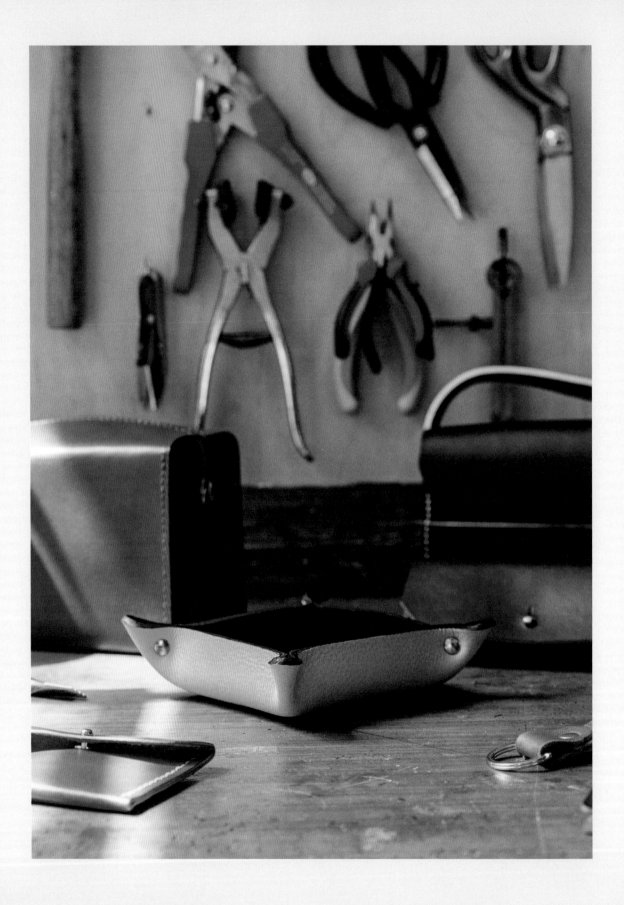

Projects

Basic techniques

For all the projects, familiarize
yourself with these techniques:

Pattern making (see p. 20)
Cutting with a knife (see p. 24)
Hammering holes, strap ends and
    corner punches (see p. 26)
Transferring the pattern
    (see p. 27)

Basic leathercraft kit

You will need the following
for all the projects:

Materials
Pattern paper or 250 gsm manilla
    card (100 lb cardstock)

Tools
Pencil
Utility knife or scalpel
Clicking knife or scalpel
Cutting mat
Metal ruler
Hammering block
Mallet
Awl
Sandpaper (600–1000 grit)

Saddle stitching kit

For projects that require saddle
stitching, you will need:

Materials
Waxed thread

Tools
Divider
Mallet
Scissors
2 harness needles
Stitch pony (optional)
Pricking chisel, 4–5-mm
    ($^{3}/_{16}$–¼-in) stitch length unless
    specified otherwise

Pattern key

Seam allowance 5 mm (¼ in)
unless specified otherwise.

Skive edges 1 cm (⅜ in) from
edge and half leather thickness
unless specified otherwise.

— —   Fold line
------   Stitch line
X   Prick mark
■   Skive edge

Headphones Tidy

- -

Basic leathercraft kit (see p. 41)

Materials
Vegetable-tanned leather,
    at least 2 mm (5 oz) thickness
Edge paint
1 Sam Browne stud
    (medium-size bulb)
Superglue

Tools
3-mm (⅛-in) hole punch
1-cm (⅜-in) hole punch

Techniques
Basic techniques (see p. 41)
Cutting small rounded corners
    (see p. 25)
Edge painting (see p. 34)
Attaching a Sam Browne stud
    (see p. 37)

Avoid tangled wires with a headphones tidy. Simply wrap the wire around the case and attach it to your bag strap or belt loop using the stud closure.

This is the perfect first project for a beginner leatherworker. It will help you grow accustomed to essential tools, including the clicking knife, awl and hole punch. No hand stitching is needed; instead you will focus on honing your cutting precision and hammering pressure. Choose a thick vegetable-tanned leather and paint the edges for an extra pop of colour.

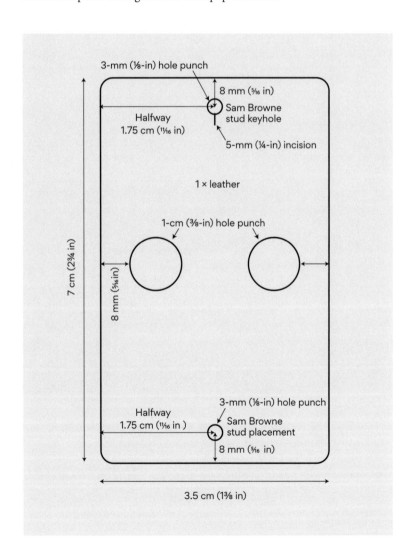

3-mm (⅛-in) hole punch

8 mm (⁵⁄₁₆ in)

Sam Browne
stud keyhole

Halfway
1.75 cm (¹¹⁄₁₆ in)

5-mm (¼-in) incision

1 × leather

1-cm (⅜-in) hole punch

7 cm (2¾ in)

8 mm (⁵⁄₁₆ in)

3-mm (⅛-in) hole punch

Halfway
1.75 cm (¹¹⁄₁₆ in)

Sam Browne
stud placement

8 mm (⁵⁄₁₆ in)

3.5 cm (1⅜ in)

Method

1. Create the pattern

Draw the pattern onto pattern paper and cut out its shape using the knife and metal ruler. Use your hole punch set to make the 1-cm (⅜-in) and 3-mm (⅛-in) circular holes.

- - - - - - - -

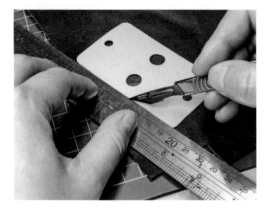

2. Cut the leather

Place the pattern on the grain side of the leather and cut out the overall rectangular shape with the knife. Score the rounded corners with the awl. Remove the pattern and cut out the rounded corners.

- - - - - - - -

3. Transfer the markings

Place the pattern back on the grain side of the leather and hammer out the holes. Remove the pattern. To create the keyhole, angle the blade at 45 degrees to the surface and make a 5-mm (¼-in) incision from the top of the keyhole line down towards the hole, as shown on the pattern.

- - - - - - - -

4. Sand down the leather

Using the sandpaper, sand down the edges of the leather to create a smooth edge. This will get rid of any stray fibres so that, when the edge paint is applied, you will achieve a smooth coloured edge.

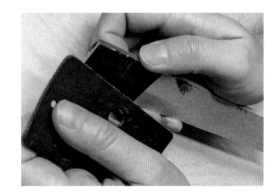

- - - - - - - -

5. Paint the edges

Using the awl, apply the edge paint around the edges of the leather. Wipe away any excess paint that has dribbled down the front or back with a dry tissue. Allow to dry.

- - - - - - - -

6. Attach the closure

To close the headphones tidy, use a Sam Browne stud. Place the screw thread through the small hole from the grain side. Apply a small amount of superglue at the top of the screw thread, and then twist on the bulb on the back side of the leather to secure it in place.

- - - - - - - -

Customization

Make this design your own by adjusting the width and length to change the size. If you have cables that are longer or thicker than average, you'll benefit from making it slightly larger. This design uses a Sam Browne stud as a closure, but feel free to experiment and try a different closure, such as a snap button. You could also burnish the edges rather than painting them for a smoother finish.

Keyring

Basic leathercraft kit (see p. 41)

Materials
Vegetable-tanned leather, at least
    2.5 mm (6 oz) thickness
Gum tragacanth
1 split ring (2.5 cm/1 in wide)
1 × 6-mm (¼-in) stem standard rivet
    (cap in the size of your choice)

Tools
3-mm (⅛-in) hole punch
Strap cutter (optional)
Beveller
Small brush
Leather-palm glove
Rivet setter

Techniques
Basic techniques (see p. 41)
Cutting rounded corners (see p. 24)
Cutting a strap/belt (see p. 25)
Bevelling (see p. 33)
Burnishing straps (see p. 34)
Setting a standard rivet (see p. 35)

This is a great project to try out the strap cutter tool, as well as burnishing with a leather-palm glove.

If you don't have a strap cutter, you can also measure out the leather for the keyring with a ruler and cut it with a knife.

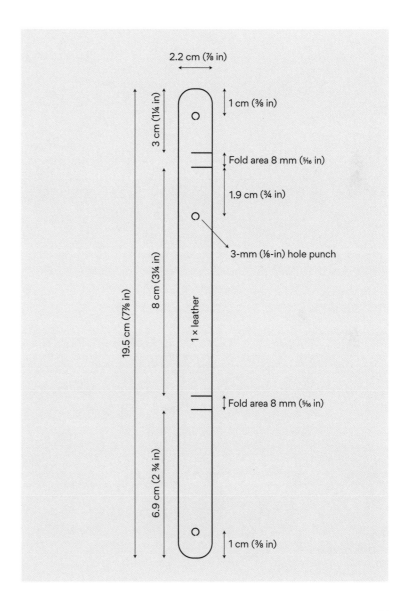

2.2 cm (⅞ in)

3 cm (1¼ in)

1 cm (⅜ in)

Fold area 8 mm (⁵⁄₁₆ in)

1.9 cm (¾ in)

3-mm (⅛-in) hole punch

19.5 cm (7⅞ in)

8 cm (3¼ in)

1 × leather

Fold area 8 mm (⁵⁄₁₆ in)

6.9 cm (2 ¾ in)

1 cm (⅜ in)

Method

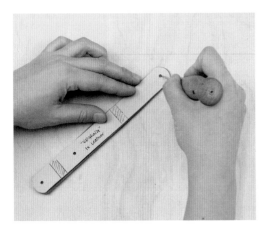

1. Create the pattern and prepare the leather

Draw and cut out your pattern, then use the hole punch to make the holes. Either place the pattern on top of the leather and cut around it with the knife or, if you have one, use a strap cutter set to 2.2 cm (⅞ in) and cut a strip of leather to the correct length. Place your pattern over the strip and mark the hole positions with the awl. Score around the curved ends, then cut these with the knife. Hammer the holes using the mallet and hole punch.

- - - - - - - -

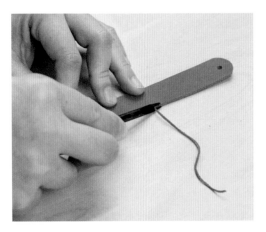

2. Bevel the edges

Bevel the edge of the leather with the beveller and sand down to create a smooth, rounded edge.

- - - - - - - -

3. Burnish the edges

Apply gum tragacanth to all the edges using a small brush. Using your leather-palm glove, burnish the edges of the leather to achieve a glossy, glazed edge. Rub the ends with your thumb to glaze the rounded ends.

- - - - - - - -

4. Attach the split ring

Insert the leather strap into the split ring, which should be positioned in the fold that is between two holes. Fold the opposite end of the strap over and align the holes, then fold the other end over the split ring, aligning the hole with the other two. Insert the stem of the rivet through the holes on one side and cap it on the other.

- - - - - - - -

5. Set the rivet

Place the rivet on top of the rivet setter on the correct size groove, and the setter over the top before hammering down with force to set the rivet in place.

- - - - - - - -

Customization

There are several ways to customize the keyring and make it your own. I have chosen to burnish the edges of this project, but you could edge paint. The length of the keyring can be altered to your taste, or you could increase the width if you wish and use a larger split ring.

Table Tray

Basic leathercraft kit (see p. 41)

Materials

Vegetable-tanned leather, at least
    1.8 mm (4½ oz) thickness –
    choose a relatively stiff leather
Suede, approximately 1.4 mm
    (3½ oz) thickness
Leather glue
Edge paint
Gum tragacanth (optional)
4 × 8-mm (5/16-in) stem standard
    rivets (cap size of your choice)

Tools

3-mm (⅛-in) hole punch
Plastic paddle
Roller
Small brush (optional)
Beveller (optional)
Burnisher (optional)
Rivet setter
Palm hammer

Techniques

Basic techniques (see p. 41)
Cutting small rounded corners
    (see p. 25)
Gluing (see p. 28)
Edge painting (see p. 34)
Bevelling (optional, see p. 33)
Burnishing (optional, see p. 33)
Setting a standard rivet (see p. 35)

This vegetable-tanned leather table tray features a suede interior to create a more refined finish.

If you choose to use it as a jewellery tray, the suede will also keep your jewellery cushioned. This project will allow you to practise the application of a thin layer of leather glue before joining the two pieces together to create a smooth surface.

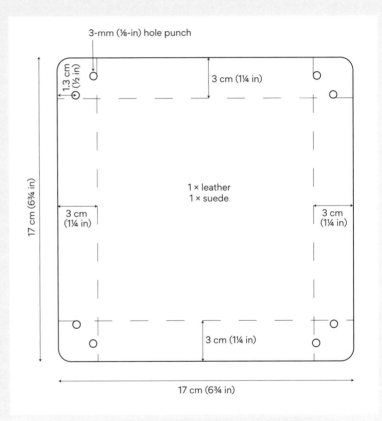

3-mm (⅛-in) hole punch

1.3 cm (½ in)

3 cm (1¼ in)

17 cm (6¾ in)

1 × leather
1 × suede

3 cm (1¼ in)

3 cm (1¼ in)

3 cm (1¼ in)

17 cm (6¾ in)

Method

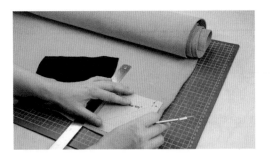

1. Create the pattern and prepare the leather

Draw and cut out the pattern and punch out the holes. Using the pattern as a guide, roughly cut the leather and suede about 1 cm (⅜ in) larger on all sides, so that you can glue the pieces together before cutting the final shape; this will enable you to achieve a clean-cut edge in the later steps.

2. Glue the layers together

With the grain sides facing down, cover the whole of the back of the leather and suede with a thin, even layer of glue. Wait for about a minute until the leather glue is tacky, then join the leathers. Roll them out flat with your roller to ensure there are no lumpy bits sandwiched in between.

3. Cut the leather

Place your pattern on top of the grain side of the vegetable-tanned leather and cut around it with your clicking knife or scalpel. Take care to keep your knife blade perpendicular to the cutting mat to ensure that you are cutting straight down into the thickness of both the vegetable-tanned leather and the suede. Cut the small rounded corners. Mark the holes with the awl and hammer them out with the hole punch.

----

4. Edge paint or burnish

If you wish to edge paint, first sand off any glue that may have squeezed out between the layers. Apply the edge paint with the awl.

If you would like to burnish the edges instead of painting them, bevel the edges of the vegetable-tanned leather only. The fibres of the suede are not dense enough to allow a clean bevel. Then apply gum tragacanth to the joined suede and vegetable-tanned leather edges and burnish them with a burnisher.

- - - - - - - -

5. Set the rivets

To create the tray shape, pinch each corner together with the vegetable-tanned leather on the outside of the tray, and use your rivet setter and mallet to secure it with a rivet. Once all the rivets are set, hammer the folded edges lightly with a palm hammer to reinforce the box shape.

- - - - - - - -

Customization

The design of the table tray is relatively simple. All you need is to decide on is the size of the tray base, then add a consistent height to all sides to attain your overall pattern. You can make it small to fit coins or jewellery, or turn it into a paper tray by making it as large as standard letters and documents.

Cardholder/Coin Purse

Basic leathercraft kit (see p. 41)
Saddle stitching kit (see p. 41)

Materials
Vegetable-tanned leather, at least
2 mm (5 oz) thickness
1 Sam Browne stud
(with medium-size bulb)
Superglue
Edge paint
Leather glue

Tools
3-mm (⅛-in) hole punch
Silver pen
Beveller (optional)
Palm hammer
Plastic paddle

Techniques
Basic techniques (see p. 41)
Cutting rounded corners
(see p. 24)
Attaching a Sam Browne stud
(see p. 37)
Bevelling (optional, see p. 33)
Edge painting (see p. 34)
Glueing (see p. 28)
Saddle stitching (see p. 29)

Keep your pennies safe with this streamlined essential. The pouch boasts plenty of space for keys, coins or cards.

Hand stitching is useful not only as a means to construct and strengthen a design but also to add visual appeal. This project demonstrates saddle stitching – a traditional technique and an essential leatherworking skill.

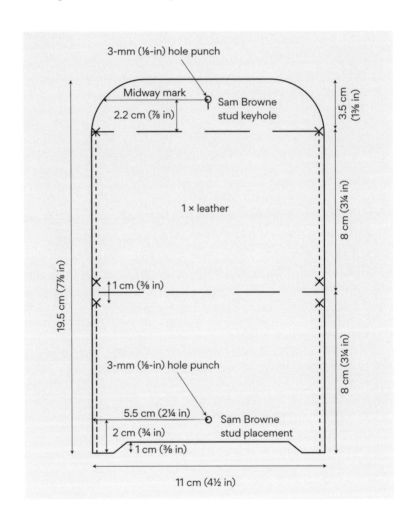

3-mm (⅛-in) hole punch

Midway mark

Sam Browne
stud keyhole

2.2 cm (⅞ in)

3.5 cm (1⅜ in)

1 × leather

8 cm (3¼ in)

19.5 cm (7⅞ in)

1 cm (⅜ in)

3-mm (⅛-in) hole punch

8 cm (3¼ in)

5.5 cm (2¼ in)

Sam Browne
stud placement

2 cm (¾ in)

1 cm (⅜ in)

11 cm (4½ in)

Method

1. Create the pattern and cut the leather

Make the pattern by cutting out the overall rectangle first before drawing in the rounded corners and indents and cutting these out with your utility knife or scalpel. Draw in any prick marks and make the holes on the pattern using the correct size of hole punch. Place the pattern on the grain side of the leather and cut around the edges using the clicking knife or scalpel. Mark the placement of the holes, prick marks and fold line. Punch the holes and make the keyhole for the Sam Browne stud.

2. Prepare to saddle stitch

Using a divider set to 5 mm (¼ in), score a line from prick mark to prick mark as indicated on the pattern. Using a pricking chisel and mallet with the leather on the hammering block, hammer the stitch holes in preparation for saddle stitching.

3. Attach the stud

Place the screw thread part of the Sam Browne stud through the hole from back of the leather. Then apply a drop of superglue to the screw thread before twisting on the bulb to secure it.

4. Paint the edges

Sand down the edges with sandpaper to smooth out any
loose fibres. If you wish to bevel the edges first to create
a more rounded edge, do that now. Using the awl, apply
the edge paint. Allow the paint to dry.

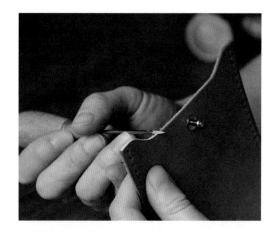

- - - - - - - -

5. Saddle stitch

Along the stitch edges, apply a layer of glue 5 mm (¼ in) in
width to the back using a plastic paddle. Once tacky, fold the
piece at the middle fold line, and align the first hole at the top
of the purse to the top edge of the inside. Hammer the fold
and glued edges gently with a palm hammer. The stitch holes
should be aligned. With harness needles and waxed thread,
saddle stitch one side from top to base. Begin by pushing one
needle through the first hole from the back of the purse to
the front. Loop over the top edge of the inside of the purse
by bringing this needle to the second hole from the front to
back. Saddle stitch down to the base of the purse. Back stitch
two stitches and hide the threads in the seam before cutting
off. Repeat on the other side. Press down the top fold, and
hammer this down gently with the palm hammer.

- - - - - - - -

Customization

Personalize this design by adjusting the width and length to change the size. Make it small to fit your
earphones or large enough to be used as a clutch. This design uses a Sam Browne stud as a fastening,
but feel free to experiment and try a different type of closure such as a magnet or buckle.

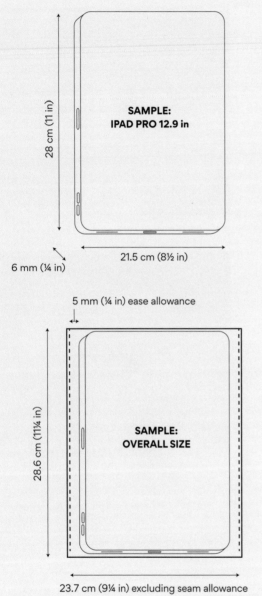

28 cm (11 in)

SAMPLE:
IPAD PRO 12.9 in

21.5 cm (8½ in)

6 mm (¼ in)

5 mm (¼ in) ease allowance

28.6 cm (11¼ in)

SAMPLE:
OVERALL SIZE

23.7 cm (9¼ in) excluding seam allowance

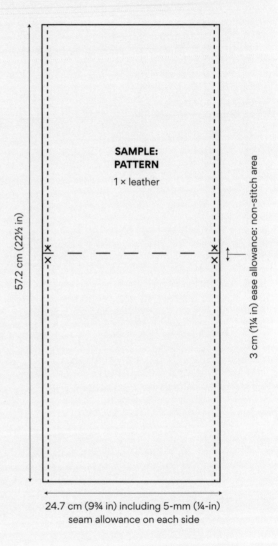

57.2 cm (22½ in)

SAMPLE:
PATTERN

1 × leather

3 cm (1¼ in) ease allowance: non-stitch area

24.7 cm (9¾ in) including 5-mm (¼-in)
seam allowance on each side

Laptop/Tablet Sleeve

Basic leathercraft kit (see p. 41)
Saddle stitching kit (see p. 41)

Materials
Vegetable-tanned leather, at least
    2 mm (5 oz) thickness (choose
    a soft, pliable leather to allow it
    to mould to your laptop/tablet)
Edge paint
Leather glue

Tools
Silver pen
Plastic paddle
Roller

Techniques
Basic techniques (see p. 41)
Edge painting (see p. 34)
Gluing (see p. 28)
Saddle stitching (see p. 29)

This is a great first made-to-measure project: you will create your pattern according to the size of your laptop or tablet.

Laptops and tablets are now so slim and lightweight that we tend to carry them around with all of our other essentials rather than in dedicated laptop bags. A protective sleeve is a perfect accessory to add to your everyday items.

Method

- - - - - - - - - - - -

1. Work out the pattern dimensions

If you have the manufacturer's measurements for your tablet or laptop you could use these, but round them to the nearest millimetre or eighth of an inch for ease of calculation and marking out the pattern. Otherwise, measure the size of your laptop or tablet, to the nearest millimetre or eighth of an inch. I made a sleeve for an iPad Pro, which has a width of 21.5 cm (8½ in), a length of 28 cm (11 in) and a depth of 6 mm (¼ in).

To find the width of the leather piece for your sleeve, add together the width, two times the depth, plus 2 cm (¾ in). This allows for a 5-mm (¼-in) seam allowance, plus 5 mm (¼ in) ease on either side for the device to slip in and out of the sleeve easily.

For the length of your sleeve, add the length of the tablet or laptop to the depth. In this instance, the finished sleeve has a width of 24.7 cm (9¾ in) and a length of 28.6 cm (11¼ in). To achieve the full pattern size, use the finished sleeve width and double the finished sleeve length to get 57.2 cm (22½ in).

- - - - - - - -

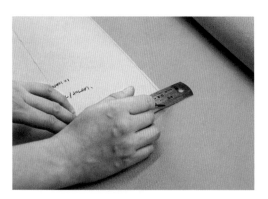

2. Create the pattern and cut the leather

It is essential to create a perfect rectangle with perpendicular corners so that when it folds up, it is not skewed. To do this, follow the pattern-making steps on pages 20–2, and pencil in the prick marks and fold line as indicated on the pattern on page 58. Place the pattern on top of the grain side of the leather and cut the straight edges. Transfer the markings for the prick marks and fold line to the leather.

- - - - - - - -

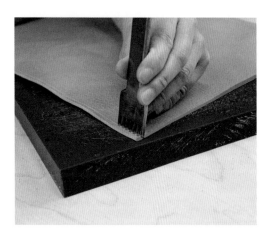

3. Prepare for saddle stitching

Set your divider to 5 mm (¼ in) and score the stitch lines. Place the first prong of the pricking chisel off the top edge of the leather and follow the score line to the prick mark at the fold. Repeat on the other edge. Now turn the entire piece around so that you start hammering holes from the bottom edge towards the centre of the piece. This will ensure that the stitch holes line up when the leather is folded.

- - - - - - - -

4. Edge paint the opening

I chose to leave the edges angular and not bevelled. Sand them down slightly to smooth out any stray fibres, then apply the edge paint to the top and bottom edges using the awl.

- - - - - - - -

5. Saddle stitch

On the back of both stitch sides, apply a thin layer of glue about 5 mm (¼ in) in width from the edge. Once the glue is tacky, fold the piece along the fold line and join the edges, making sure the sides are flush. Use a roller to squeeze out any excess glue. Cut a piece of waxed thread 4–5 times the length of the stitch line (from the opening of the sleeve to the folded base) and thread the needles. Start saddle stitching from the opening side of the sleeve so that the ends of the thread will sit at the base, where they will experience less pulling. Double up the first stitch by looping it twice over the painted edge for extra strength. Repeat for the other side.

- - - - - - - -

6. Final edge paint

Sand down the stitched edges slightly to smooth out any excess glue. Using the awl, apply edge paint in a colour of your choice. Allow the paint to dry before adding another coat. Once the paint has dried, the sleeve is ready to use.

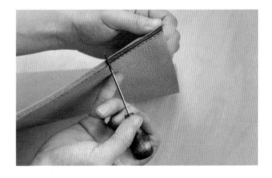

- - - - - - - -

Customization

You can add various front or back pockets for your business cards or documents, or even attach a deep pocket to hold your charger. Another great addition to the sleeve is to add loops to the front so that you can attach extra cables. Refer to the intermediate Cable Organizer project (see p. 82) to incorporate these details.

Passport Holder

Basic leathercraft kit (see p. 41)

Saddle stitching kit (see p. 41)

Materials
Vegetable-tanned leather,
    at least 2 mm (5 oz) thickness
Gum tragacanth
Leather glue

Tools
Silver pen
Beveller
Small brush
Burnisher
Plastic paddle
Roller

Techniques
Basic techniques (see p. 41)
Cutting rounded corners (see p. 24)
Bevelling (see p. 33)
Burnishing (see p. 33)
Gluing (see p. 28)
Saddle stitching (see p. 29)

The minimalist design of this passport holder will keep your passport and boarding pass protected without feeling like you are carrying extra baggage.

With the sheer number of things we carry in our hand luggage nowadays, I wanted something that wouldn't be cumbersome. It is difficult to achieve a clean cut on rounded corners, so I have chosen to burnish the edges to smooth out any messy cuts.

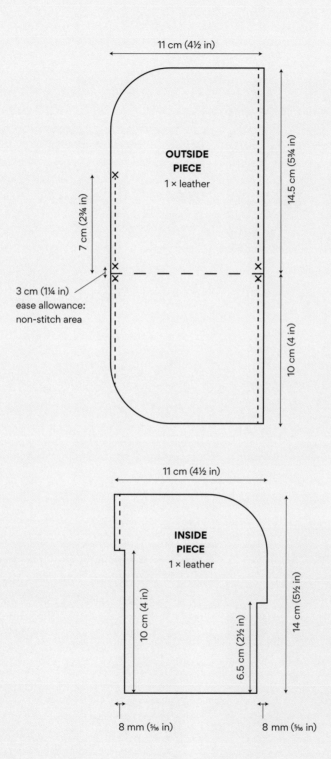

11 cm (4½ in)

OUTSIDE PIECE
1 × leather

14.5 cm (5¾ in)

7 cm (2¾ in)

3 cm (1¼ in)
ease allowance:
non-stitch area

10 cm (4 in)

11 cm (4½ in)

INSIDE PIECE
1 × leather

10 cm (4 in)

6.5 cm (2½ in)

14 cm (5½ in)

8 mm (⁵⁄₁₆ in)

8 mm (⁵⁄₁₆ in)

Method

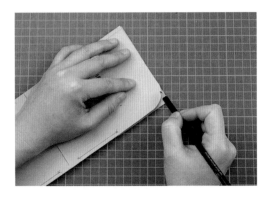

1. Create the pattern and cut the leather

Treat the two pattern pieces as rectangles and cut out their overall size first. Draw in and cut out the rounded corner on the inside piece. With this as a template, trace the same shape onto the outside piece and cut out. Mark the prick marks and fold line. Place the inside and outside pattern pieces on the grain side of the leather. Cut out the shapes, and mark the prick marks and fold line.

- - - - - - - -

2. Bevel and burnish the edges

Bevel all edges and sand down all sides of both pieces. Apply gum tragacanth to the top edge of the inside piece and the top and bottom edges of the outside piece, including the rounded corners, then burnish these edges with your burnisher. Leave the stitch edges unburnished at this stage.

- - - - - - - -

3. Hammer holes with the pricking chisel

Using the divider, score the stitch lines on the grain side of the leather. Place the inside piece grain side up, with the rounded edge at the top. Allow the first prong of your pricking chisel to sit off the top left edge and hammer down this line. Place the outside piece grain side up. Start at the top right corner, with the first prong of your pricking chisel off the edge. Hammer down until you reach the prick mark. Jump over the gap and place the first prong of the pricking chisel on the next prick mark. Hammer until you reach the bottom edge. Move to the left side of the outside piece. Place the first prong of the chisel on the prick mark below the fold and hammer to the curved edge. Swivel the outside piece 180 degrees, and place the first prong of the chisel on the prick mark below the fold of the final score line. Hammer 7 cm (2¾ in) to the next prick mark.

4. Glue the pieces

Using the plastic paddle, apply a thin layer of glue about 5 mm (¼ in) wide on the edge on the back of the pieces where you have created holes for stitching.

Place the outside piece back side up. Once the glue is tacky, turn the inside piece over, so that the grain side is facing up, and stick it down, aligning the top left corner of the inside piece to the top left corner of the outside piece. Fold up the outside piece at the fold line, as indicated on the pattern, and glue down the remaining edges, making sure the sides are flush. Use a roller to roll down the edges and squeeze out any excess glue.

- - - - - - - -

5. Saddle stitch, sand down and burnish

Starting at the top on the straight edge, saddle stitch your way down to the fold. On the other side, start saddle stitching at the curve and make your way to the fold. Finish off each stitch line by hiding the ends in between the seams.

Sand down the stitch sides to get rid of excess glue and create a smooth, rounded finish. Apply gum tragacanth to the stitched edges with a small brush and burnish the sides with the burnisher. You will see the fibres coming together to reveal one smooth, glazed edge.

- - - - - - - -

Customization

The best way to customize this project is to add extra card slots to the front or back. Simply cut a rectangle slightly larger than a card size and stitch this to the front or back piece of the holder before you assemble it. Otherwise, use different-coloured leather to differentiate the separate sections.

Keychain Lanyard

Basic leathercraft kit (see p. 41)

Materials
Vegetable-tanned leather,
    at least 2 mm (5 oz) thickness
Edge paint
2 × 7-mm (¼-in) stem standard
    rivets (5-mm/¼-in cap size)
1 split ring (2.5 cm/1 in wide)

Tools
1-cm (⅜-in) hole punch
3-mm (⅛-in) hole punch
Silver pen
Strap cutter
Beveller
Leather-palm glove
Rivet setter

Techniques
Basic techniques (see p. 41)
Cutting a strap/belt (see p. 25)
Edge painting (see p. 34)
Bevelling (see p. 33)
Burnishing straps (see p. 34)
Setting a standard rivet (see p. 35)

This is one of my favourite accessories: a keychain lanyard designed to be worn around the neck.

The leather case around the keys helps protect your clothes and stops any noisy jangling as you move. This design explores a very interesting way to create a three-dimensional shape without stitching and it is good practice for working with an irregular pattern piece.

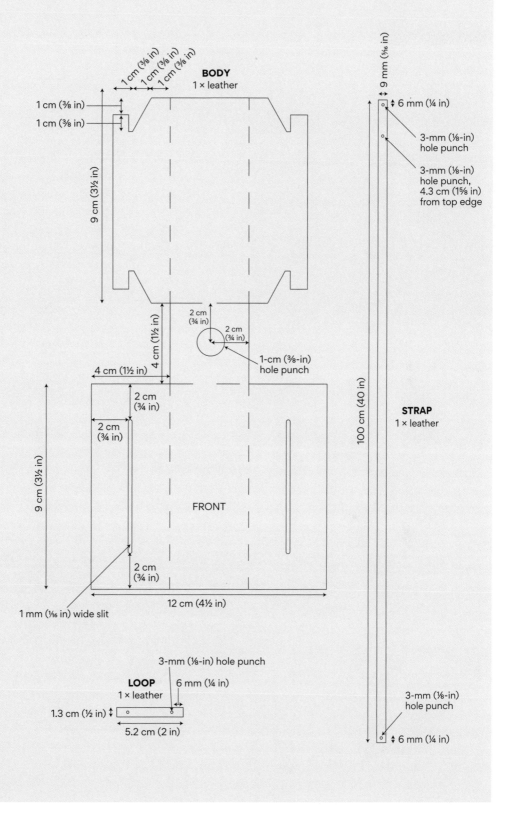

BODY
1 × leather

1 cm (⅜ in)
1 cm (⅜ in)
1 cm (⅜ in)

1 cm (⅜ in)

1 cm (⅜ in)

9 cm (3½ in)

2 cm (¾ in)

2 cm (¾ in)

1-cm (⅜-in) hole punch

4 cm (1½ in)

4 cm (1½ in)

2 cm (¾ in)

2 cm (¾ in)

9 cm (3½ in)

FRONT

2 cm (¾ in)

12 cm (4½ in)

1 mm (1⁄16 in) wide slit

LOOP
1 × leather

3-mm (⅛-in) hole punch

6 mm (¼ in)

1.3 cm (½ in)

5.2 cm (2 in)

9 mm (⁵⁄16 in)

6 mm (¼ in)

3-mm (⅛-in) hole punch

3-mm (⅛-in) hole punch, 4.3 cm (1⅝ in) from top edge

100 cm (40 in)

STRAP
1 × leather

3-mm (⅛-in) hole punch

6 mm (¼ in)

Method

1. Make the pattern pieces

The best way to make the body pattern is to cut the overall rectangle to 12 × 22 cm (4½ × 8½ in) before cutting into it to create the unusual shape. Hammer the hole using a 1-cm (⅜-in) hole punch and cut the incisions. Place your pattern on the grain side of the leather and cut the overall size as you have done with the pattern, then score around the pattern using an awl. Remove the pattern and cut out the shape. Punch out the 1-cm (⅜-in) hole and make the incisions. For the strap, cut a straight edge approximately 100 cm (40 in) long. Make this longer or shorter depending how you like to wear it. Cut the strap with a strap cutter. Cut out the strap loop using a knife. Punch out the holes on the strap and strap loop.

- - - - - - - -

2. Edge paint, and bevel and burnish the strap

Sand down the edges of the body and strap loop. Apply the edge paint on all the outside edges of the body and all around the strap loop and wait for it to dry before applying second or third coat if you wish, to make the colour more vibrant.

As the strap is to be worn around the neck, bevel the edges with a beveller and burnish them with a leather-palm glove so that the strap will feel smooth upon the skin.

- - - - - - - -

3. Connect the sides

Once your leather is cut and the edges are finished, slot the sides of the body together to create the three-dimensional shape.

- - - - - - -

4. Secure the loop

Wrap the strap loop around so that the holes meet. Secure with a rivet by slotting the stem of the rivet through the holes and capping it. To set it, cut a small scrap of leather to fit inside the loop under the rivet. As the rivet setter will not fit inside the loop, place the setter on top of the rivet and hammer down. Remove the scrap leather. Pull both ends of the strap through the loop, aligning the single hole at one end with the hole 4.3 cm (1⅝ in) from the other end.

- - - - - - - -

5. Attach the strap to the body

Push the strap ends through the hole at the top of the body until they appear on the other side.

- - - - - - -

6. Set the rivet

Similar to the Keyring project (see p. 46), thread one end of the strap through the split ring, wrap it around and fold over to allow the three holes on the strap ends to meet. Insert the stem of the rivet into the holes on one side and cap it on the other. Set this on the rivet setter. Put your keys onto the split ring and push the case down to hide the keys.

- - - - - - -

Customization

Depending on the number of keys you'd like to carry with you, you can customize your lanyard by expanding its width and depth. The best way to do this is to create a prototype with your pattern paper to see whether the dimensions are correct before moving on to the leather.

Glasses Case

Basic leathercraft kit (see p. 41)
Saddle stitching kit (see p. 41)

Materials
Vegetable-tanned leather,
    at least 2 mm (5 oz) thickness
Edge paint
1 Sam Browne stud
    (with medium-size bulb)
2 × 6-mm (¼-in) stem standard
    rivets (cap size of your choice)
Superglue
Leather glue

Tools
Silver pen
Palm hammer or roller
3-mm (⅛-in) hole punch
Paring knife
Granite/marble block
Plastic paddle
Rivet setter

Techniques
Basic techniques (see p. 41)
Skiving (see p. 26)
Edge painting (see p. 34)
Setting a standard rivet (see p. 35)
Attaching a Sam Browne stud
    (see p. 37)
Gluing (see p. 28)
Saddle stitching (see p. 29)

The glasses case is a perfect object to explore an unusual triangular gusset.

The gusset creates interior volume and a rigidity that will keep your glasses safe and protected from being squashed in your bag.

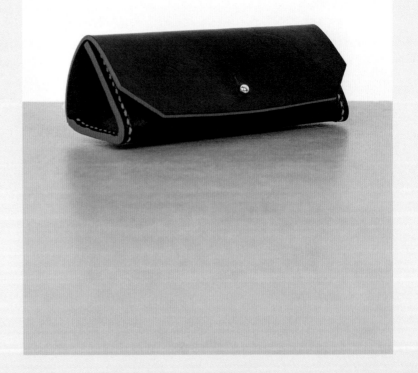

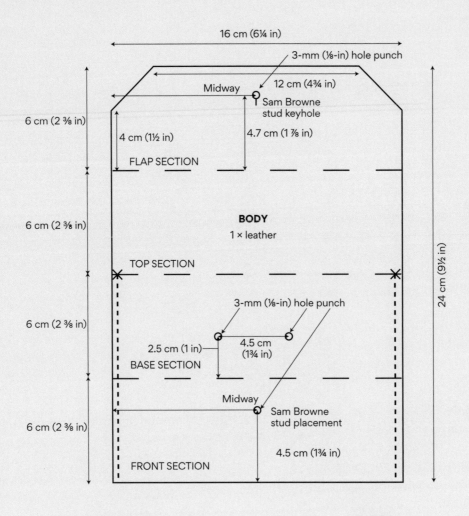

16 cm (6¼ in)

3-mm (⅛-in) hole punch

12 cm (4¾ in)

Midway

Sam Browne
stud keyhole

6 cm (2 ⅜ in)

4 cm (1½ in)

4.7 cm (1 ⅞ in)

FLAP SECTION

6 cm (2 ⅜ in)

BODY
1 × leather

24 cm (9½ in)

TOP SECTION

3-mm (⅛-in) hole punch

6 cm (2 ⅜ in)

2.5 cm (1 in)

4.5 cm
(1¾ in)

BASE SECTION

Midway

Sam Browne
stud placement

6 cm (2 ⅜ in)

4.5 cm (1¾ in)

FRONT SECTION

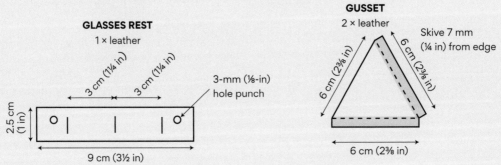

GLASSES REST
1 × leather

3 cm (1¼ in)   3 cm (1¼ in)

3-mm (⅛-in)
hole punch

2.5 cm
(1 in)

9 cm (3½ in)

GUSSET
2 × leather

Skive 7 mm
(¼ in) from edge

6 cm (2⅜ in)

6 cm (2⅜ in)

6 cm (2⅜ in)

Method

1. Prepare the pattern and cut the leather

Create and cut out the pattern pieces, marking the relevant prick marks and punching the holes. Label each section on the body pattern piece. Place the pattern pieces on the grain side and cut the leather pieces. Before removing the pattern, make the prick marks with the awl. Mark the ends of the fold line with a silver pen on the back of the leather. Hammer the creases gently with a palm hammer or roller.

Skive the edges on the gussets as indicated on the pattern. Punch the holes on the base and front sections of the body. To create the keyhole for the Sam Browne stud, punch a 3-mm (⅛-in) hole on the flap, as shown by the pattern. Then, using a clicking knife, make a 5-mm (¼-in) incision, slicing downwards towards the hole.

2. Prepare for saddle stitching

On the body and gussets, score the stitch lines with the divider. Turn the body so that the front section is at the top. Hammer the holes for stitching, starting at the front section edge of the body. Allow the first prong of the pricking chisel to hang off the edge and hammer your way to the prick mark. Repeat this on the other side. Likewise, on the gussets, hammer the two stitch sides, starting with the first prong off the edge of the leather.

3. Edge paint

Sand down the edges to create smooth edges on all of the pieces. Edge paint the edges that do not need to be stitched.

4. Attach the glasses rest

Attach the glasses rest to the body using rivets. The glasses rest is positioned inside the body, so slot the stem of the rivet from the grain side of the body through to the glasses rest and secure it with the cap. Secure with the rivet setter, then repeat for the other side of the rest.

5. Attach the Sam Browne stud

Place the screw thread of the Sam Browne through the hole in the front section of the body from the back side of the leather and out the front. Add a small amount of superglue to the tip and screw on the bulb.

6. Glue the gussets

Add a 5-mm (¼-in) width of glue along the back of the stitch edges of the body and gussets. Once the glue is tacky, glue the gusset to the body and push the seam of the gusset into the fold of the base and front sections so that it sits flush. Attach the other gusset in the same way.

7. Saddle stitch gussets to body

Start the saddle stitching at the front section edge. Loop both ends of the thread over this edge and through the first stitching hole to strengthen this opening before continuing to saddle stitch. When you reach the fold between the front and base sections, stitch as follows: take the needle from the body side through the stitch hole and out at the corner of the gusset. Then take the needle on the gusset side and push this into the corner and out the hole on the body that the previous needle has just come out of. Continue to saddle stitch as normal until you reach the end of the stitch line. Back stitch twice before bringing both needles through the seam and hiding the ends of the thread in the seam. Repeat on the other side.

- - - - - - - -

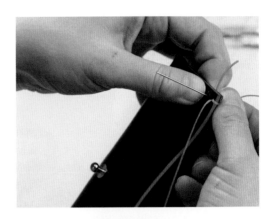

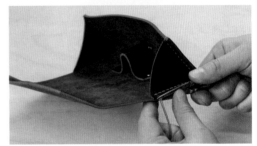

8. Final edge paint

Sand down the stitched sides so that they are smooth and appear as one clean edge. Apply edge paint to finish off the stitched edges. Once the paint dries, your glasses case is ready to use.

- - - - - - - -

Customization

This design is for a relatively large pair of glasses. However, you could customize it by changing the size. To do so, decide on the length of the gusset and change the sides of the equilateral triangle accordingly. Then alter the flap, back, base and front to match this new size. Another way to customize the glasses case is to refer to the Wristlet project (see p. 88) and add a wrist strap to one side that could potentially attach to the side of a bag.

Belt

Basic leathercraft kit (see p. 41)
Saddle stitching kit (see p. 41)

Materials

Vegetable-tanned leather, at least
    3 mm (7½ oz) thickness
Gum tragacanth
3.2-cm (1¼-in) buckle
Leather glue

Tools

Measuring tape
Strap cutter
Paring knife
Granite/marble block
5-mm (¼-in) hole punch
2.5-cm (1-in) long crew punch
Beveller
Small brush
Leather-palm glove
Plastic paddle

Techniques

Basic techniques (see p. 41)
Cutting a strap/belt (see p. 25)
Skiving (see p. 26)
Bevelling (see p. 33)
Burnishing straps (see p. 34)
Gluing (see p. 28)
Saddle stitching (see p. 29)

This simple belt is one of the few projects that does not require a pattern but will still fit perfectly on the person you are making it for.

You will learn how to attach a buckle – a technique that you can use to make adjustable straps or closures for bags.

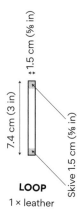

LOOP
1 × leather

7.4 cm (3 in)
↕1.5 cm (⅝ in)
Skive 1.5 cm (⅝ in)

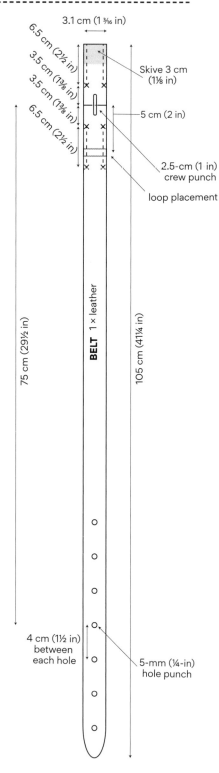

3.1 cm (1 ³⁄₁₆ in)
6.5 cm (2½ in)
3.5 cm (1⅜ in)
3.5 cm (1⅜ in)
6.5 cm (2½ in)

Skive 3 cm (1⅛ in)
5 cm (2 in)
2.5-cm (1 in) crew punch
loop placement

75 cm (29½ in)

BELT 1 × leather

105 cm (41¼ in)

4 cm (1½ in) between each hole

5-mm (¼-in) hole punch

Method

1. Work out the belt length and width

It is not completely necessary to make a pattern for this project. However, the pattern diagram on page 76 serves as a guide to show you where to place the prick marks and holes.

Use a measuring tape to find the circumference of your waist. For this example, I will work with 75 cm (29½ in). For the buckle side of the belt, add an additional 10 cm (3⅞ in) for the attachment of the buckle. For the other end, add another 20 cm (7⅞ in) to allow room for adjustments. The overall length of the belt in this example is 105 cm (41¼ in).

A buckle size is identified by its inner width, excluding the metal parts. The width of your belt should be 1 mm (1/16 in) less than the inner width of your buckle. This allows you to slide the belt into the buckle without damaging the edges of the leather. The buckle I will use has an inner width of 3.2 cm (1¼ in); therefore, I will make a belt with a width of 3.1 cm (1³/16 in).

For this belt, I made a 1.5 cm (⅝ in) wide loop. To find the length of the loop, add together 2 times the belt width and 4 times the thickness of the leather: $(2 \times 3.1 \text{ cm}/1^3/_{16}\text{in}) + (4 \times 3 \text{ mm}/\frac{1}{8}\text{ in})$. The loop for this belt will be 7.4 cm (3 in) long.

- - - - - - - -

2. Cut the leather

Place the leather on the cutting mat and, using your clicking knife, cut a straight edge on a side slightly longer than 105 cm (41¼ in). Adjust the strap cutter to 3.1 cm (1³/16 in) and cut your belt piece.

At one end of the belt cut a clean straight edge. Skive off approximately 3 cm (1¼ in) from the edge of this end. At the other end of the belt, mark 105 cm (41¼ in) or the intended length and score in a dome shape using the awl. Cut around this neatly. Cut the loop and skive off approximately 1.5 cm (⅝ in) on both ends.

- - - - - - - -

3. Punch the holes and hammer the stitch holes

Use a metal ruler and awl to mark out the position of the crew punch, belt loop and other prick marks, as shown on the diagram. Use the divider to create the score lines for stitching from prick mark to prick mark. With the pricking chisel, hammer down the holes in preparation for saddle stitching. Follow the measurements shown on the diagram and punch out the crew punch where the buckle will be attached, using the same method as for punching holes.

As my belt is for a 75-cm (29½-in) waist, one of the holes should give a perfect fit. To achieve this, measure 75 cm (29½ in) from the centre of the crew punch towards the tail end of the belt. Use an awl to make a mark before punching the first 5-mm (¼-in) hole here. From this point, make two or three more holes on either side, 4 cm (1½ in) apart, to allow for adjustment.

- - - - - - - -

4. Bevel and burnish the edges

Bevel the edges of the belt with the beveller and sand down to create a smooth, round finish. You may choose to bevel both the grain and back sides of the leather. An efficient way to apply the gum tragacanth is to roll up the leather and apply a layer of gum tragacanth with a small brush on all the edges. Use the leather-palm glove to burnish the edges of the belt.

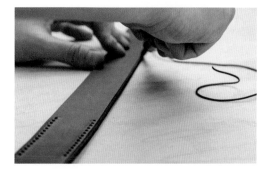

- - - - - - - -

5. Attach the buckle and loop

Attach the buckle by slotting the belt through it and pulling the pin through the crew punch hole. Then attach the loop. Apply a small amount of glue on the skived edges of the loop. Add the same amount on the back of the leather at the position where the loop will be attached. This loop should be approximately 5 cm (2 in) from the buckle. Once the glue is tacky, glue down the loop so that it is joined on the back. Once the loop is secured, glue down the stitch edges of the belt to set in place the loop and buckle, while making sure the stitch holes are aligned.

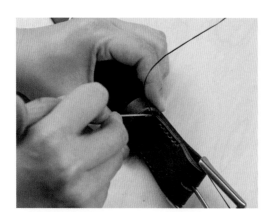

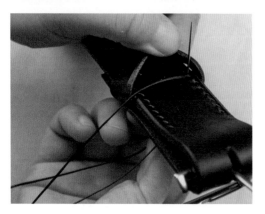

6. Saddle stitch

Begin saddle stitching close to the buckle. On your first stitch, you could loop around the edge of the leather a couple of times for extra strength and to create a visual feature. Continue saddle stitching down to the loop. Once you reach the loop, take an awl and push through the stitch holes so that the awl creates holes through the loop in the same place. Then manoeuvre the needles under the loop to continue saddle stitching.

----

7. Finish stitching

Once you arrive at the end of this first stitch line, make sure both needles are on the back of the belt. Grab both needles and threads and twist, creating a twisted line across the width of the leather. Once you have reached the other side, push one needle through from the back to the grain side in the last stitch hole, and the other one in the second to last stitch hole. Continue to saddle stitch back up towards the buckle and finish off by hiding the ends in the seam.

- - - - - - - -

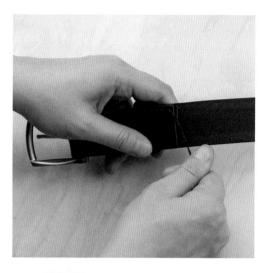

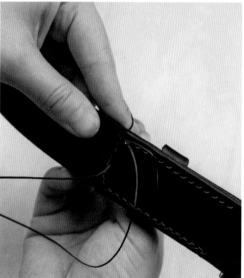

Customization

There is a myriad of buckle designs out there, so the best way to customize this project is to choose a different buckle for your belt. Buckle widths vary, so you will need to make sure you adjust the width of your belt accordingly. For a more hardwearing piece, a solid brass buckle is best.

Cable Organizer

Basic leathercraft kit (see p. 41)
Saddle stitching kit (see p. 41)

Materials
Vegetable-tanned leather,
    at least 2 mm (5 oz) thickness
    (choose a soft leather)
1.5-cm (⅝-in) wide hook-and-loop
    tape in lengths of:
    - 5 cm (2 in) (loop side –
      2 pieces)
    - 10 cm (4 in) (hook side)
    - 12.5 cm (5 in) (loop side)
    - 16.5 cm (6½ in) (hook side)
Superglue
Edge paint
Leather glue
16-mm (¼-in) stem standard rivet
    (cap size of your choice)

Tools
Paring knife
Granite/marble block
Silver pen
Roller
Palm hammer
Plastic paddle
Rivet setter

Techniques
Basic techniques (see p. 41)
Skiving (see p. 26)
Edge painting (see p. 34)
Gluing (see p. 28)
Saddle stitching (see p. 29)
Setting a standard rivet (see p. 35)
Tacking (see p. 32)

With our ever-expanding collections of phones, laptops, tablets and even toothbrushes that require cables, it is not unusual for the wires to end up in a tangled mess.

To cater for both the light and heavy electronic traveller, I have designed the cable organizer with hook-and-loop tape closures, to allow the organizer to contract or expand.

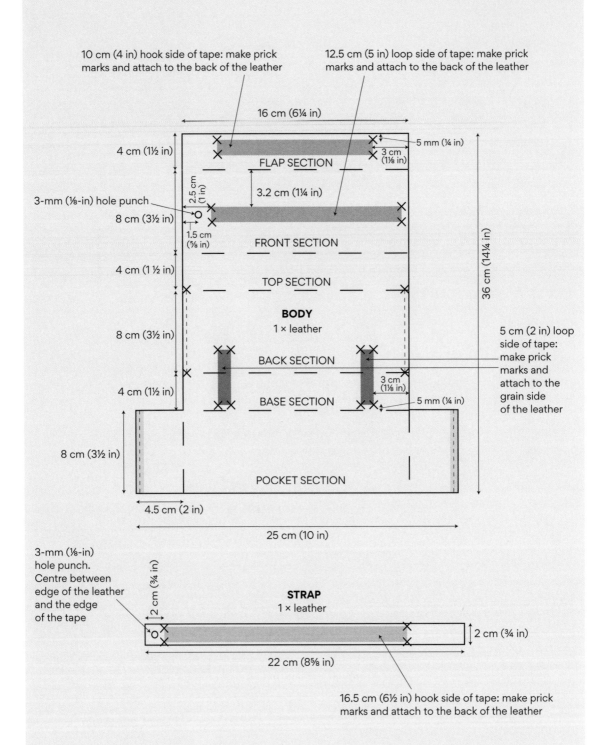

10 cm (4 in) hook side of tape: make prick marks and attach to the back of the leather

12.5 cm (5 in) loop side of tape: make prick marks and attach to the back of the leather

16 cm (6¼ in)

4 cm (1½ in)

5 mm (¼ in)

3 cm (1⅛ in)

FLAP SECTION

2.5 cm (1 in)

3.2 cm (1¼ in)

3-mm (⅛-in) hole punch

8 cm (3½ in)

1.5 cm (⅝ in)

FRONT SECTION

36 cm (14¼ in)

4 cm (1 ½ in)

TOP SECTION

BODY
1 × leather

8 cm (3½ in)

5 cm (2 in) loop side of tape: make prick marks and attach to the grain side of the leather

BACK SECTION

3 cm (1⅛ in)

4 cm (1½ in)

BASE SECTION

5 mm (¼ in)

8 cm (3½ in)

POCKET SECTION

4.5 cm (2 in)

25 cm (10 in)

3-mm (⅛-in) hole punch. Centre between edge of the leather and the edge of the tape

2 cm (¾ in)

STRAP
1 × leather

2 cm (¾ in)

22 cm (8⅝ in)

16.5 cm (6½ in) hook side of tape: make prick marks and attach to the back of the leather

Method

----

1. Create the pattern, cut the leather and mark the hook-and-loop tape placement

Make your pattern and place it on top of the grain side of the leather. Cut out your leather pieces. Skive the edges of the body as indicated on the pattern. Transfer the prick marks using an awl and mark the ends of the fold lines with a silver pen. There are many prick marks to be made, so take care to mark them in the correct place. Using a roller or a palm hammer, make the creases for the folds. Place each of the hook-and-loop tape pieces on the leather, taking care to follow the pattern for accurate placement. Use an awl or silver pen to mark the four corners of each piece on the leather. Note which pieces go on the grain side and which go on the back before marking.

----

2. Attach the hook-and-loop tape

Apply superglue to the back of each tape piece and attach it to the leather. Run the roller over the tape and immediately wipe away any excess glue with a clean, dry cloth. Allow the glue to dry before moving on to the next step.

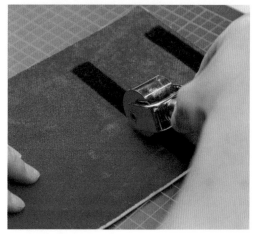

----

3. Edge paint

Sand down the edges to create smooth surfaces on all your pieces and apply edge paint to all sides apart from the stitch edges, which will be painted at the end.

4. Prepare the edges and saddle stitch

Before stitching, reinforce the folds with a palm hammer. Score in the stitch lines with the divider, as indicated on the pattern, and hammer down the stitch holes from prick mark to prick mark with the pricking chisel. For the lines that begin on the edge of the leather, start with the first prong of the chisel hanging off the edge and hammer your way down. Apply a thin layer of leather glue about 5 mm (¼ in) wide on the back of the stitch edges and join together once the glue is tacky. Roll over these edges with the roller to set.

Starting at the top of the pocket section, saddle stitch towards the base section and finish off by hiding the thread ends in the seam. Repeat on the other side.

5. Edge paint stitched edges

Sand down the stitched edges before applying edge paint. Once this is dry, apply a second coat if you wish to have a thicker layer of paint.

----

6. Attach hook-and-loop tape strap

Attach the hook-and-loop tape strap by sandwiching together the body and strap with a rivet. Secure it with a rivet setter. Tack both sides of the other end of the hook-and-loop tape strap to give it a more secure grip, as this is the puller for releasing the strap.

7. Tack the corners (optional)

This creates a finished corner that is both a design feature and protects the corners from wear and tear. Fold down the corners and create two holes through both layers using your awl. Loop the thread through two of the holes and make a double knot on the back to hide the thread ends before tacking the corner down.

- - - - - - - -

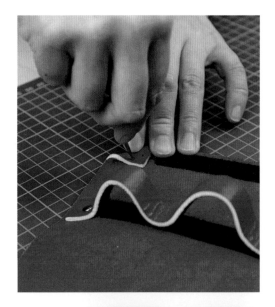

Customization

Two great ways to customize the cable organizer are to make a more compact version by either taking out the pocket and adding another attachment for cables or to make it into a flat pocket. It really depends on what you need to fit in there, and you can change the interior position of the features to whatever is most useful for you.

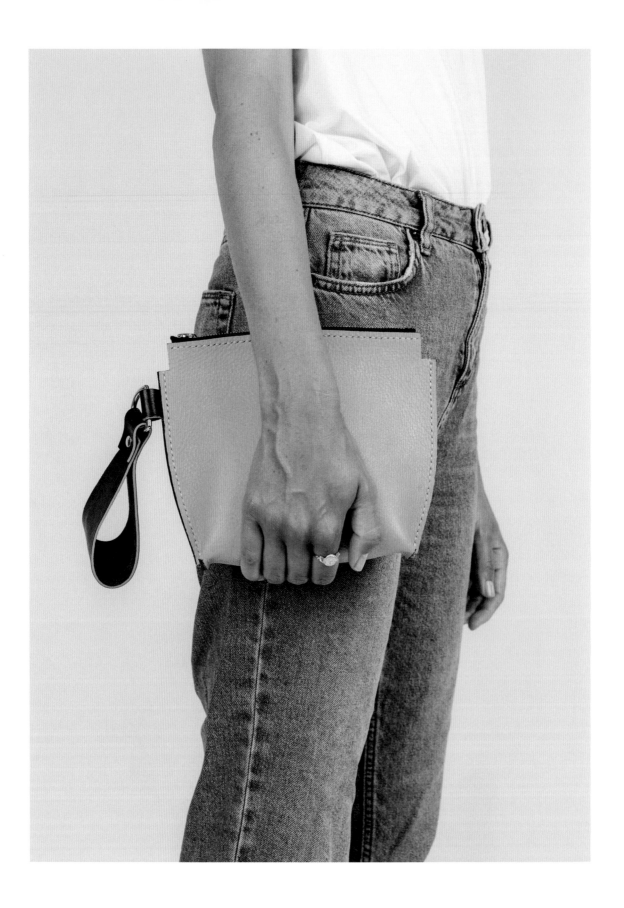

Wristlet

Basic leathercraft kit (see p. 41)
Saddle stitching kit (see p. 41)

Materials
Vegetable-tanned leather,
    at least 2 mm (5 oz) thickness
Edge paint
Leather glue
2.5-cm (1-in) D-ring
1 × 19-cm (7½-in) zip
1 × 7-mm (¼-in) stem standard
    rivet (cap size of your choice)

Tools
3-mm (⅛-in) hole punch
Silver pen
Palm hammer
Paring knife
Granite/marble block
Plastic paddle
Roller
Rivet setter

Techniques
Basic techniques (see p. 41)
Skiving (see p. 26)
Edge painting (see p. 34)
Gluing (see p. 28)
Saddle stitching (see p. 29)
Setting a standard rivet (see p. 35)

This simple wristlet is an introduction to the T-base, which is a classic way to create a three-dimensional shape from one piece of leather.

The T-base is aptly named to indicate the shape it makes when the sides are sewn to the base of the bag. This is also a good project to help you perfect the skill of inserting a zip.

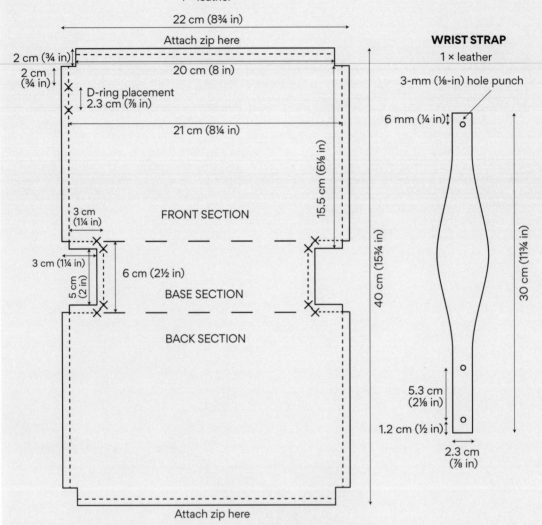

BODY
1 × leather

22 cm (8¾ in)

Attach zip here

2 cm (¾ in)

2 cm (¾ in)

20 cm (8 in)

D-ring placement
2.3 cm (⅞ in)

21 cm (8¼ in)

15.5 cm (6⅛ in)

40 cm (15¾ in)

3 cm (1¼ in)

FRONT SECTION

3 cm (1¼ in)

5 cm (2 in)

6 cm (2½ in)

BASE SECTION

BACK SECTION

Attach zip here

WRIST STRAP
1 × leather

3-mm (⅛-in) hole punch

6 mm (¼ in)

30 cm (11¾ in)

5.3 cm (2⅛ in)

1.2 cm (½ in)

2.3 cm (⅞ in)

D-RING ATTACHMENT
1 × leather

2.3 cm (⅞ in)

Skive 8 mm (⁵⁄₁₆ in)

5 cm (2 in)

Method

1. Create the pattern and cut the leather

Make your pattern. In this design I have created a rounded and wider wrist strap as a feature, but you could make it straight. Whichever style you choose, make sure the width of the strap ends is always a little smaller than the internal width of the D-ring.

Place your pattern on the grain side of the leather and cut out your pieces. For the curved wrist strap, it is easier to score the shape onto the leather with an awl, then remove the pattern and cut out its shape. Make the prick marks and hammer the holes with the hole punch. Use a silver pen to mark the ends of the fold lines, and fold and hammer these gently with a palm hammer. Skive the sides of the D-ring attachment.

2. Edge paint

There will be two stages of edge painting for this project, as the stitched edges can only be painted after stitching. Sand down the sides of all three pieces until smooth. Paint the edges of the wrist strap and D-ring attachment using an awl. Edge paint the two zip attachment edges of the body, as it will be difficult to paint these edges once the zip is in place.

3. Glue and attach the D-ring

Put your D-ring attachment through the D-ring, with the grain side facing outwards. Apply leather glue with a small paddle or brush to the skived areas and press them together. Using your awl, scratch the hide side of the skived area of the D-ring attachment to create a rough surface before sticking this between the prick marks on the body.

4. Hammer the holes for saddle stitching

Using the divider, score the stitch lines as indicated on the pattern. Use the pricking chisel to create stitch holes for both sides of the zip. Then place the body grain side up in front of you, with one zip edge on top and the other at the bottom. Hammer the holes for the side seams, starting at the top left side with the first prong of the pricking chisel sitting off the top edge and hammering down the score line. Turn the corner and continue until you reach the next corner at the prick mark. Jump over that prick mark to the next one and hammer the line at the base section of the body, stopping at the prick mark. Repeat from the top right of the body to the base section. Turn the body 180 degrees, so that the back section of the body is at the top. Repeat what you did on the other side, beginning with the pricking chisel hanging off the top edge and finishing at the base section.

- - - - - - - -

5. Attach the zip

With the zip closed, fold the ends over to hide the frayed edges, and to fit into the opening. To do so, apply glue to the ends and fold them in so that the frayed edges are hidden. Apply a layer of glue approximately 5 mm (¼ in) wide to the back side of the zip-attachment edge of the body. Place the zip attachment edge of the leather onto the fabric of the zip, leaving a gap of around 3 mm (⅛ in) in between the teeth of the zip and the edge of the leather.

Saddle stitch the zip to the body down the stitch line on the side you have glued. Glue and then stitch the other zip attachment edge of the leather to the zip. The best way to go about this is to roll the leather with the zip on top and allow the other zip attachment edge to meet the zip.

- - - - - - - -

6. Saddle stitch and edge paint the sides

To assemble the wristlet, glue the sides together by applying glue to the back of the seam allowance on the stitch edges. Press together, ensuring the edges are flush, and run the roller over the edge to set it. Do the same on the other side. Starting at the top, saddle stitch your way down towards the base section and hide the thread ends in the seam. To create the T-base, apply glue to the back of the seam allowance on the stitch edges at the base section and press them together. Saddle stitch to finish the construction. Repeat this on the other side.

Sand down the stitched sides to remove any excess glue and to create a smooth finish. Then edge paint these sides to finish off the body of the bag.

- - - - - - - -

7. Attach the wrist strap

To attach the wrist strap, pull the end that has two holes through the D-ring, and wrap the end around it so that the two holes align. Pull the other end of the wrist strap down and slot it in between so that all three holes are aligned. Place a rivet through these three holes and cap it on the other side before setting it with the rivet setter.

- - - - - - - -

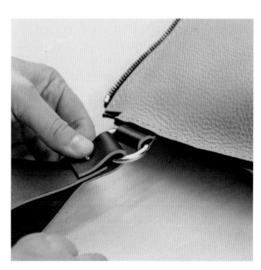

Customization

You can make a smaller version to be used as a make-up bag or an extra-large design to create a clutch. Either way, all you need to do is change the dimensions to fit to your needs. Another option is to add a long strap to make it into an over-the-shoulder bag.

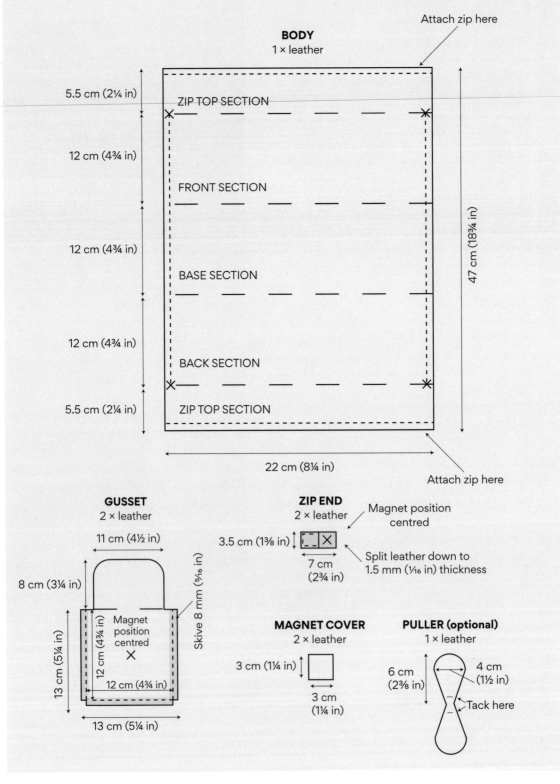

BODY
1 × leather

Attach zip here

5.5 cm (2¼ in)

ZIP TOP SECTION

12 cm (4¾ in)

FRONT SECTION

12 cm (4¾ in)

BASE SECTION

12 cm (4¾ in)

BACK SECTION

5.5 cm (2¼ in)

ZIP TOP SECTION

47 cm (18¾ in)

22 cm (8¼ in)

Attach zip here

GUSSET
2 × leather

11 cm (4½ in)

8 cm (3¼ in)

Skive 8 mm (⁵⁄₁₆ in)

13 cm (5¼ in)

12 cm (4¾ in)

Magnet position centred
X

12 cm (4¾ in)

13 cm (5¼ in)

ZIP END
2 × leather

Magnet position centred

3.5 cm (1⅜ in)

7 cm (2¾ in)

Split leather down to 1.5 mm (¹⁄₁₆ in) thickness

MAGNET COVER
2 × leather

3 cm (1¼ in)

3 cm (1¼ in)

PULLER (optional)
1 × leather

6 cm (2⅜ in)

4 cm (1½ in)

Tack here

Toiletry Bag

Basic leathercraft kit (see p. 41)
Saddle stitching kit (see p. 41)

Materials
Vegetable-tanned leather,
    at least 2 mm (5 oz) thickness
Edge paint
Leather glue
2 snap closure magnets
    (no larger than 2.5 cm/1 in)
32-cm (12½-in) zip

Tools
Silver pen
Palm hammer
Paring knife
Granite/marble block
Beveller (optional)
Another pricking chisel, 3-mm
    (⅛-in) stitch length
Plastic paddle
Lighter
Roller
Pliers (optional)

Techniques
Basic techniques (see p. 41)
Cutting rounded corners
    (see p. 24)
Skiving (see p. 26)
Edge painting (see p. 34)
Bevelling (optional, see p. 33)
Saddle stitching (see p. 29)
Attaching a snap closure magnet
    (see p. 38)
Tacking (optional, see p. 32)

This is a practical, durable and stylish bag for all your essentials that introduces you to the box shape design.

I have created extended flaps to the gusset, which helps to keep all the items in. It also includes a long zip to enable you to open the bag wide.

Method

1. Create the pattern and cut the leather

Make the pattern pieces and place them on the grain side of the leather. Cut out the pieces. Transfer the markings and skive the edges of the gussets. Hammer down the folds using a palm hammer. The pattern includes instructions to split the zip ends. Splitting is a way of reducing the thickness of the leather uniformly. Make sure your paring knife is sharp and place the leather on top of a granite or marble block. Start at the midway point of the back of one zip end. Press down one side of the leather with your fingers and, with the other hand, run the paring knife from the mid-point towards the other side in a zig-zag movement until the uppermost layer of the leather is off. Keep the knife relatively flat in order to take off an even thickness. Turn the piece around and repeat on the other side.

- - - - - - - -

2. Edge paint

Sand down the edges of the leather pieces. If you prefer a more rounded look, you can run a beveller along all the edges before you sand them. Now paint the edges of all the pieces apart from the sides that will be stitched.

- - - - - - - -

3. Prepare for saddle stitching

Using the divider, score the stitch lines as indicated on the pattern, taking care to score within the prick marks on the body. Use the larger pricking chisel to hammer down the holes between the prick marks on the sides. On the zip top section of the body, start chiselling by placing the first prong of the chisel off the edge of the leather and continue along the score line. For the gusset, place the first prong of the chisel off the top edge and follow the score line down to the bottom. Jump across to the other side, leaving the baseline till last.

- - - - - - - -

4. Attach the magnet

On the gusset, make two 5-mm (¼-in) incisions on either side of the magnet placement, about 1 cm (⅜ in) apart. Slot the metal prongs of the female part of the magnet through these incisions and hammer down the prongs so that they fold towards each other on the back. Place the magnet cover over the back of the magnet and score around it with an awl. Using a plastic paddle, apply a thin layer of glue within these score lines, as well as on the back of the magnet cover piece. Once the glue is tacky, stick the magnet cover over the back of the magnet. Repeat this on the other gusset.

- - - - - - - -

5. Attach the zip ends

Attach the male parts of the magnets to the grain side of the zip ends. The process is the same as for attaching the female parts. Once each magnet is in place, apply leather glue to the entire back of the zip end, as well as to the fabric end of the zip, starting at the metal teeth. Once the glue is tacky, sandwich the fabric end of the zip by folding the zip end over it, making sure the magnet is facing down. Repeat on the other end of the zip.

Using the divider, score the lines around the zip ends, as indicated on the pattern. Using the smaller pricking chisel, hammer the stitch holes all the way through the layers.

- - - - - - - -

6. Stitch the zip ends

Take approximately 30 cm (12 in) of waxed thread and saddle stitch around the first zip end. Then back stitch two stitches and finish off with the thread ends on the back. Cut off at the tip and melt off the thread ends with a lighter. Repeat on the other side.

7. Attach the zip

Centre the zip on the zip top section of the body and mark its position on the zip fabric with a silver pen. Apply a thin layer of glue to the back, about 5 mm (¼ in) wide, across the zip top section edge. Lay this over the zip and glue in position. Leave approximately 3 mm (⅛ in) between the zip teeth and the edge of the leather. Roll over the edge with a roller to set it. Allow the glue to dry, then saddle stitch the glued side of the zip in place. Repeat on the other side.

- - - - - - - -

8. Attach the gusset

Gently reinforce the folds of the body with the palm hammer before attaching the first gusset. Using the plastic paddle, apply a 5-mm (¼-in) width of glue to the back of the stitch edges of the body and gusset. Once this is tacky, glue the gusset to the body, taking care at the corners to ensure that it sits neatly in the fold.

- - - - - - - -

9. Stitch the gusset, sand down and edge paint, and attach the puller

Measure a length of waxed thread that is 4–5 times the total length of one stitched side. Begin saddle stitching this side from the top of the gusset. When you reach the corner, take the needle from the body side into the corner. Then take the needle from the gusset side into the corner and out of the same hole that the other needle has just come from. Then continue as normal. Once you have reached the end, back stitch a couple of stitches and hide the thread ends in the seam. Repeat steps 8 and 9 to complete the other gusset side of the bag. Sand down the stitched edges before applying edge paint.

If your zip does not have a puller, create one by cutting the puller pattern piece and using it to cut the leather. Make sure the folded part fits within the width of the ring on your zip. Sand down and edge paint this piece. Fold it in half and tack just beneath the fold. Pull open the ring with pliers, slot in the leather puller and close the ring again with pliers.

- - - - - - - -

Customization

A great way to customize the toiletry bag is to apply a different type of closure. To do this, take out the zip and extend the top so that it folds over on itself. Use a snap button or magnet to close. You can also easily add a small handle or change it into a handbag by adding a long strap. To do so, attach a D-ring to either side and cut a long strap to attach to these, following the instructions in the Crossbody Bag project (see p. 112).

Large Wallet

Basic leathercraft kit (see p. 41)

Saddle stitching kit (see p. 41)

Materials
Vegetable-tanned leather,
    1.25 mm (3 oz) thickness
    (choose a relatively stiff
    leather for this project)
Edge paint
Leather glue
14-cm (5½-in) zip

Tools
4 bulldog clips (optional)
Silver pen
Paring knife
Granite/marble block
Palm hammer
Pricking chisel,
    3-mm (⅛-in) stitch length
Plastic paddle
Roller

Techniques
Basic techniques (see p. 41)
Skiving (see p. 26)
Edge painting (see p. 34)
Saddle stitching (see p. 29)

In this project you will create a classic wallet with card slots and a zip purse for coins.

The concertina gusset allows the inner pockets to expand to fits lots of cards, notes and coins, yet also slim down when the wallet is not full. There are five pattern pieces, so make sure you label them all correctly.

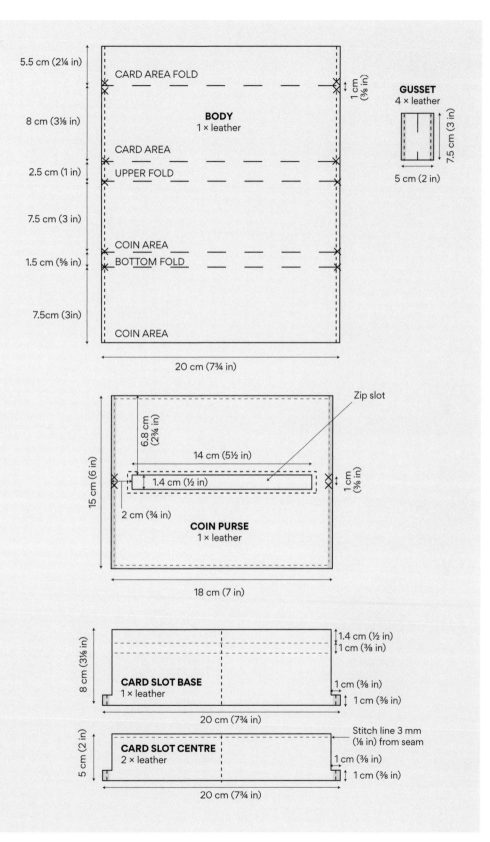

BODY
1 × leather

5.5 cm (2¼ in)

CARD AREA FOLD

1 cm (⅜ in)

8 cm (3⅛ in)

CARD AREA

UPPER FOLD

2.5 cm (1 in)

7.5 cm (3 in)

COIN AREA

BOTTOM FOLD

1.5 cm (⅝ in)

7.5cm (3in)

COIN AREA

20 cm (7¾ in)

GUSSET
4 × leather

7.5 cm (3 in)

5 cm (2 in)

Zip slot

6.8 cm (2¾ in)

14 cm (5½ in)

1.4 cm (½ in)

1 cm (⅜ in)

15 cm (6 in)

2 cm (¾ in)

COIN PURSE
1 × leather

18 cm (7 in)

8 cm (3⅛ in)

1.4 cm (½ in)

1 cm (⅜ in)

CARD SLOT BASE
1 × leather

1 cm (⅜ in)

1 cm (⅜ in)

20 cm (7¾ in)

5 cm (2 in)

CARD SLOT CENTRE
2 × leather

Stitch line 3 mm (⅛ in) from seam

1 cm (⅜ in)

1 cm (⅜ in)

20 cm (7¾ in)

Method

- - - - - - - - - - -

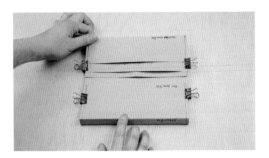

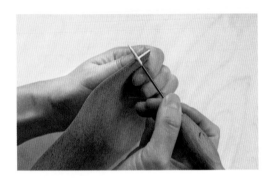

1. Prepare the pattern and cut the leather

Create and cut out the pattern pieces. You may want to use the pattern pieces as a prototype – in which case, bulldog clip the sides to check all the lengths are correct and the edges are flush. Mark the required stitch lines, folds and prick marks on your pattern pieces as indicated. Place the pattern pieces on the grain side of the leather and cut out. Take extra care to be precise in your cutting for this project, as the pieces will need to fit perfectly for a clean finish. Transfer the markings and skive the pieces as indicated on the pattern.

- - - - - - - -

2. Edge paint

You will need to paint several edges before assembling your wallet. Sand down and paint the top and bottom of the body, the bottom edge of the card slot base and both card slot centre pieces, the zip slot of the coin purse and the top edge of all of the gussets. Allow the paint to dry.

- - - - - - - -

3. Prepare the coin purse

Before inserting the zip, use a divider to score the stitch line around the zip slot and the other edges of the coin purse. Take note of the prick marks you've transferred from the pattern. Use the pricking chisel to hammer down the stitch holes along these score lines.

The zip should fit directly into the zip slot. Apply a 5-mm (¼-in) wide strip of leather glue to the back edges of this slot. Place the zip face up on the table, then lay the leather piece over the zip so that it fits into the slot. Hammer down gently with a palm hammer and allow the glue to dry and set for 2–3 minutes. Saddle stitch the zip to the leather. Once completed, apply a 5-mm (¼-in) strip of glue to the back of the top and bottom stitch line edges that run parallel to the zip. Fold the coin purse over so that the zip sits on top and the glued edges are flush. Saddle stitch the bottom of the purse to secure it, but leave the sides until the next step.

- - - - - - - -

4. Attach the gussets and edge paint

Using the divider, score a stitch line down the longer edges of each gusset. Starting with the painted edge at the top, hammer down each stitch line with the pricking chisel. Allow the first prong of the chisel to hang off the top edge.

Apply a 5-mm (¼-in) strip of glue to the back of one of the stitch line edges of each gusset piece, and the side edges (front and back) of the coin purse. Once tacky, stick two gussets to the front of the coin purse and two to the back, matching up the glued edges. With the gussets glued to the coin purse, saddle stitch each side to secure. Sand down the edges before applying edge paint with an awl.

- - - - - - - -

5. Prepare the card slots

It is important that the card slots fit perfectly with no gaps. Score the 3-mm (⅛-in) seam allowance on the card slot centre pieces. Note that this is a smaller seam allowance than usual.

Place the card slot base piece in front of you, with the grain side up and the protruding "ears" of the piece closest to you. Then place one of the card slot centre pieces on top, again grain side up, with the "ears" of this piece sitting a step up from those of the base.

Using the furthest edge of the card slot centre as a guide, score a line with the awl to indicate its position on the card slot base. Secure the two pieces by applying a 2-mm (1/16-in) strip of leather glue to the back of the card slot centre, along the stitch line edge. Apply a corresponding strip of glue just below the score line you made on the card slot base. Once the glue is tacky, place the card slot centre in the correct position on the base. Following the score line on the card slot centre, hammer down stitch holes through both pieces with your pricking chisel and saddle stitch across. Once completed, attach the second card slot centre piece to the card slot base in the same way, positioning it a step up from the previous piece.

- - - - - - - -

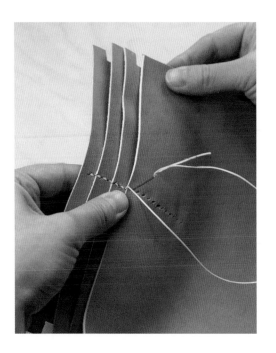

6. Join the card slots to the body

Make a strong fold 5.5 cm (2¼ in) from the top of the body, as indicated on the pattern. Reinforce the fold by using a roller to roll out the crease. Open this up again before continuing.

Lay down the assembled card slots, grain side up, and place the body over the top, aligning the left and right corners of the body a step down from the lowest "ears" of the card slots. Now divide the card slots so that your cards will fit perfectly. Score a 7.5-cm (3-in) line with your awl and metal ruler in the middle of the layered pieces, from the top of the card slots to the 5.5-cm (2¼-in) crease you've just made. Hammer the pricking chisel forcefully down this stitch line, so that it goes through all the joined pieces, and saddle stitch along this line.

- - - - - - - -

7. Join the sides of the card area

Use a divider to score the 5-mm (¼-in) seam allowance on the sides of the card slots and the body of the wallet. Turn the body around so that the coin area is at the top and the card slots are closest to you. Starting at the top, hammer down the stitch lines with a pricking chisel, letting the first prong of the chisel hang off the top edge to ensure that the first stitches are the same length. As you continue down, take note of the 1-cm (⅜-in) gap between the prick marks on the body. Jump across to continue hammering the stitch holes all the way until you reach the end of the card slots. Do the same to the other side.

Apply a 5-mm (¼-in) strip of glue to the stitch edges on the back of the leather, avoiding the space between the prick marks at the upper fold and bottom fold on the body. Once the glue is tacky, fold down the card slot area at the 5.5-cm (2¼-in) crease you made previously and align the edge of the card slots to meet at the top of the upper fold. Then guide the remaining pieces in place so that the ears fit exactly, leaving no gaps.

- - - - - - - -

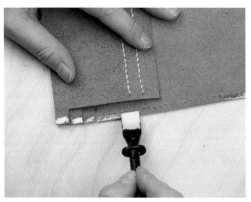

8. Attach the coin pouch

Apply glue to the back of the stitch line edges of the gussets. With care, align the top of the gussets to the top edge of the body. Glue the edges down, making sure the side edges are flush. Then fold up at the bottom fold and attach the remaining gusset edges to the body, gluing between the bottom fold and upper fold. Once glued, you will see the final shape. The coin purse is now sandwiched between two large slots for notes, and six card slots are on top. Press down at the folds by hammering lightly with the palm hammer. Saddle stitch the sides to secure.

- - - - - - - -

9. Edge paint to finish

Once stitched, sand down the sides to create a smooth edge before applying edge paint with the awl.

- - - - - - - -

Customization

If you take out the card slots and coin pouch, the concertina construction can easily turn into the gusset of a handbag/purse by simply adding a strap and a zip to close. Make it into a portrait shape, add handles and it can be turned into a tote bag. The concertina construction is so versatile and functional, it is a great design to adapt for different projects.

Shopper

Basic leathercraft kit (see p. 41)
Saddle stitching kit (see p. 41)

Materials
Vegetable-tanned leather,
    at least 2 mm (5 oz) thickness
Vegetable-tanned leather,
    at least 3 mm (7½ oz)
    thickness for straps
Gum tragacanth
2 snap closure magnets
    (size of your choice)
8 × 6-mm (¼-in) stem standard
    rivets (cap size of your choice)
Leather glue

Tools
Silver pen
3-mm (⅛-in) hole punch
Beveller
Paring knife
Granite/marble block
Small brush for gum tragacanth
Burnisher
Strap cutter
Leather-palm glove
Rivet setter
Plastic paddle

Techniques
Basic techniques (see p. 41)
Skiving (see p. 26)
Cutting a strap/belt (see p. 26)
Burnishing straps (see p. 34)
Saddle stitching (see p. 29)
Attaching a snap closure magnet
    (see p. 38)
Setting a standard rivet (see p. 35)

With its sleek silhouette, the shopper tote is the essence of both form and function. Effortlessly versatile, it offers bags of room for your possessions.

In this project, you will learn how to create a wide gusset. The design enables you to create a clean rectangular shape, and you can pull open the bag to reveal a wide boat shape.

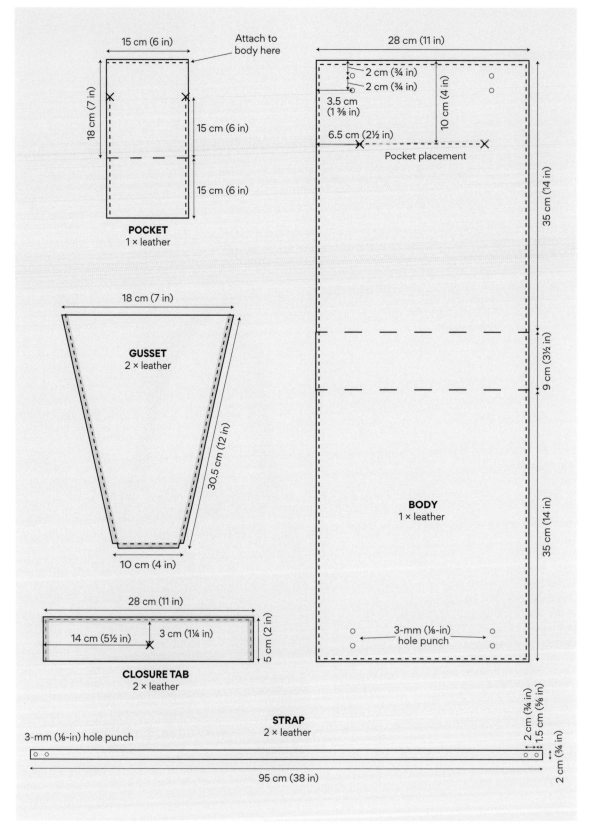

POCKET
1 × leather

15 cm (6 in)

Attach to body here

18 cm (7 in)

15 cm (6 in)

15 cm (6 in)

GUSSET
2 × leather

18 cm (7 in)

30.5 cm (12 in)

10 cm (4 in)

CLOSURE TAB
2 × leather

28 cm (11 in)

14 cm (5½ in)

3 cm (1¼ in)

5 cm (2 in)

STRAP
2 × leather

3-mm (⅛-in) hole punch

95 cm (38 in)

2 cm (¾ in)

1.5 cm (⅝ in)

2 cm (¾ in)

BODY
1 × leather

28 cm (11 in)

2 cm (¾ in)
2 cm (¾ in)

3.5 cm (1 ⅜ in)

6.5 cm (2½ in)

Pocket placement

10 cm (4 in)

35 cm (14 in)

9 cm (3½ in)

35 cm (14 in)

3-mm (⅛-in) hole punch

Method

- - - - - - - - - - -

1. Create the pattern and cut the leather

Make the patterns for all pieces apart from the straps. You will be able to use a strap cutter to cut directly into the thicker leather at a later stage. Check the surface of the thinner hide and place the body pattern on the smoothest part on the grain side, as this will be the front of the bag. Arrange the other pattern pieces around the body piece before cutting out the leather and transferring the markings.

For the gusset, cut the edges straight, then go back and cut off the corners. Punch out the holes and make the prick marks using an awl. For the body, gussets and closure tabs, score in the stitch lines with the divider and hammer the stitch holes on the grain side with a pricking chisel, always beginning with the first prong of the chisel hanging off the edge or on the prick mark to ensure correct alignment.

- - - - - - - -

2. Prepare the body, gussets and straps

Bevel all edges of the body with the beveller. Skive off approximately 1 cm (⅜ in) from the three edges of the gussets, as indicated on the pattern. Bevel and burnish the top edges. Make the straps from the thicker leather using the strap cutter. Punch the holes and bevel and burnish the strap edges. To burnish the straps, it is best to use the leather-palm glove technique.

- - - - - - - -

3. Prepare the pocket and closure tabs

Score the stitch line and hammer the stitch holes for the sides of the pocket with a pricking chisel on the grain side. Score the stitch line and hammer the stitch holes for the attachment to the body of the bag on the back side of the leather. Skive the three edges of the closure tabs, as indicated on the pattern. Then attach a magnet to each closure tab by cutting a 5-mm (¼-in) incision on each side of the magnet placement. Slot the prongs of the magnet into the slits and hammer them down on the back.

- - - - - - - -

4. Attach the straps

Matching the holes on the strap to those on the body, place the stem of the rivet from the back of the body and cap on top of the strap, sandwiching the two pieces of leather. Set the rivet. Check that it is secure before repeating for the other three rivets on this side of the bag. Repeat for the other side of the bag.

- - - - - - - -

5. Saddle stitch the pocket

Fold the pocket piece at the fold line, and saddle stitch the sides of the pocket together. Then saddle stitch the top of the pocket to the back of the body. This will be on the inside of the bag once completed.

- - - - - - - -

6. Saddle stitch the body and gussets

Using a plastic paddle, apply a 5-mm (¼-in) strip of leather glue to the back of the stitch edges on the closure tabs, body and gussets. Once the glue is tacky, join the closure tabs to the top of the body and the gussets to the sides. Squeeze the gusset corners into the folds of the base of the body to achieve neat corners. Your bag will now take on its final shape.

Cut an arm's length of thread. Starting at the top corner of the bag, saddle stitch your way down. Once you've reached the ends of the threads, hide the ends in the seam before cutting another arm's length of thread and saddle stitching from where you left off. As you stitch your way down, you will soon reach the corner of the gusset. Take the needle on the body side through the next stitch hole and into the corner of the gusset. Take the needle from the gusset side and enter the corner to come out of the same hole. Then continue to saddle stitch until you have stitched the whole bag.

----

7. Burnish the edges

To finish off the bag, sand down the stitched edges to get rid of excess glue. Apply gum tragacanth with a small brush and burnish using a burnisher.

Customization

You can customize your shopper tote by applying a different type of handle such as the rounded handle in the Weekender project (see p. 166), or the curved handle in the Wristlet project (see p. 88). Make it as functional as you like by removing the pocket or moving the pocket to the front of the bag. You can mix up the colours by using a different-coloured leather for the gussets, but make sure you use the same type and thickness of leather as the body of the bag to ensure a uniform feel throughout the design.

Crossbody Bag

- -

Basic leathercraft kit (see p. 41)
Saddle stitching kit (see p. 41)

Materials
Vegetable-tanned leather,
    at least 2 mm (5 oz) thickness
    (choose a stiff leather)
2 × 1.8-cm (¾-in) D-rings
    with detachable bars
Superglue
Edge paint
Leather glue
1 × 1.8-cm (¾-in) double slider
2 × 6-mm (¼-in) stem standard
    rivets (cap size of your choice)

Tools
Strap cutter
Silver pen
3-mm (⅛-in) hole punch
6-mm (¼-in) hole punch
Paring knife
Granite/marble block
Palm hammer
Plastic paddle
Rivet setter

Techniques
Basic techniques (see p. 41)
Cutting a strap/belt (see p. 25)
Skiving (see p. 26)
Edge painting (see p. 34)
Gluing (see p. 28)
Saddle stitching (see p. 29)
Setting a standard rivet (see p. 35)

If you are a fan of the minimalist look, this is a perfect project for you. A fabulous mini crossbody bag is ideal for a night out. The size is designed to fit a small wallet, phone, keys and any other small essentials.

This project is an introduction to the hidden gusset, which gives an elegant and structured box shape.

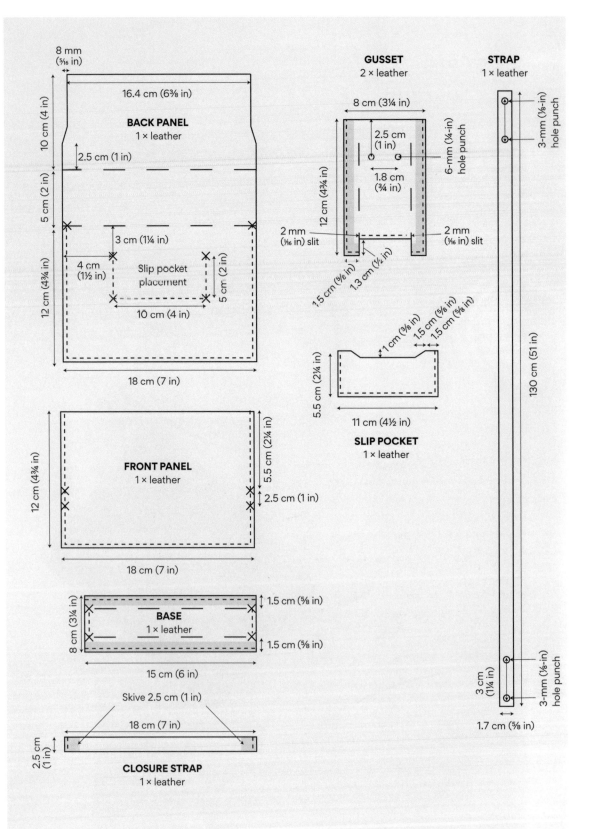

8 mm (5/16 in)

10 cm (4 in)

16.4 cm (6⅜ in)

BACK PANEL
1 × leather

2.5 cm (1 in)

5 cm (2 in)

3 cm (1¼ in)

4 cm (1½ in)

Slip pocket placement

5 cm (2 in)

12 cm (4¾ in)

10 cm (4 in)

18 cm (7 in)

FRONT PANEL
1 × leather

12 cm (4¾ in)

5.5 cm (2¼ in)

2.5 cm (1 in)

18 cm (7 in)

BASE
1 × leather

8 cm (3¼ in)

1.5 cm (⅝ in)

1.5 cm (⅝ in)

15 cm (6 in)

Skive 2.5 cm (1 in)

18 cm (7 in)

2.5 cm (1 in)

CLOSURE STRAP
1 × leather

GUSSET
2 × leather

8 cm (3¼ in)

2.5 cm (1 in)

6-mm (¼-in) hole punch

1.8 cm (¾ in)

12 cm (4¾ in)

2 mm (1/16 in) slit

2 mm (1/16 in) slit

1.5 cm (⅝ in)

1.3 cm (½ in)

1 cm (⅜ in)

1.5 cm (⅝ in)

1.5 cm (⅝ in)

5.5 cm (2¼ in)

11 cm (4½ in)

SLIP POCKET
1 × leather

STRAP
1 × leather

3-mm (⅛-in) hole punch

130 cm (51 in)

3-mm (⅛-in) hole punch

3 cm (1¼ in)

1.7 cm (⅝ in)

Method

----

1. Prepare the pattern and cut the leather

Cut out the pattern pieces as an overall rectangle first before cutting into any indents and making the 2-mm (1/16-in) slits on the gussets. The strap could be shorter or longer if you wish. Use the strap cutter to make the strap.

Once you have cut the pattern pieces and made the prick marks, transfer the pattern to the leather and cut out the pieces. Mark the edges of the fold lines with a silver pen. Make the prick marks with an awl, punch the holes and skive the closure-strap ends, gussets and base with a sharp paring knife. These are relatively long lengths to skive, so practise first on a piece of scrap leather.

----

2. Attach the D-rings to the gusset

To attach the D-ring to the gusset, separate the detachable bar of the D-ring from the loop. Slot the loop of the D-ring through the 6-mm (1/4-in) holes. From the back, slot the bar back through the D-ring and apply a small amount of superglue to the screw thread to ensure that it doesn't come out. Repeat with the second D-ring and gusset.

----

3. Edge paint, and hammer the stitch holes

Before assembling the bag, apply edge paint to the edges that do not need to be stitched. Score all the stitch lines with the divider and hammer down the stitch holes with the pricking chisel. Press down at the fold lines and hammer them gently with a palm hammer – this will make the final construction easier. For the gusset and base, the fold must be made with the grain sides facing. The back panel is to be folded with the back sides facing.

4. Attach the closure strap to the front panel

Apply a small amount of leather glue to the back of the stitch edges of the closure strap, and in between the prick marks on the grain side of the front panel. Before applying the glue to the front panel, scratch the surface slightly with an awl, as the rough surface will allow the glue to set more easily. Once the glue is tacky, stick the closure strap down.

----

5. Attach the interior slip pocket

Apply a 5-mm (¼-in) strip of leather glue along the back edges of the stitch lines of the pocket and on the back of the back panel, as marked. Once the glue is tacky, glue the slip pocket onto the back panel by aligning the top edge of the slip pocket to the first stitch hole of the pocket on the back panel. Saddle stitch together by allowing the first stitch to loop over the top of the slip pocket.

----

6. Attach the base to the gussets

Use leather glue to secure the short edge at the bottom of each gusset to the sides of the base. Saddle stitch with approximately 20 cm (8 in) of waxed thread. Once both sides are stitched, the gussets and base will appear as one long piece.

----

7. Attach the front and back panel

Before attaching the final pieces, reinforce the folds by hammering them down with the palm hammer. Then apply a thin strip of leather glue to the back of the stitch lines of the front panel, back panel and the remaining stitch lines of the gussets and base. Once the glue is tacky, stick the front panel to the gusset and base with precision, so that the edges are flush. To create a more refined look, at the base of the bag, aim for the feet of the gusset to sit neatly next to the base with only a small slit visible. Do the same to the back panel. Saddle stitch the front and back panels to complete the bag.

8. Attach the strap

To attach the adjustable strap, pull one end of the strap through the slider so that the strap wraps around its central bar. Matching the holes already made, secure it with a rivet.

Take the other end of the strap and loop it through the D-ring. Pull the strap end back towards the slider and slot it in one side and out the other. Take the other end of the strap and loop it through the D-ring on the other side of the bag. Secure with a rivet.

- - - - - - - -

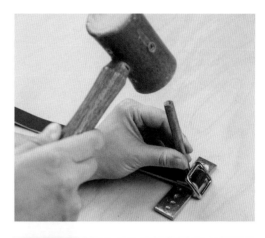

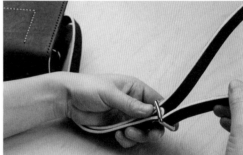

9. Final edge paint

Sand down all the stitched edges, taking care to sand away any glue that is visible to create a smooth edge. Using the awl, apply edge paint to these edges.

- - - - - - - -

Customization
Consider this as a mini version of a satchel. With that in mind, the best way to customize it is to make it large enough to fit a laptop by changing the length, width and depth.

Tote

Basic leathercraft kit (see p. 41)
Saddle stitching kit (see p. 41)

Materials
Vegetable-tanned leather,
    at least 2 mm (5 oz) thickness
Edge paint
Leather glue
Superglue
4 x 1.5 cm (⅝-in)
    diameter flat magnets
4 Sam Browne studs
    (with medium-size bulb)

Tools
Silver pen
Paring knife
Granite/marble block
Strap cutter
3-mm (⅛-in) hole punch
Beveller (optional)
Leather-palm glove (optional)
Palm hammer
Plastic paddle
1–2 bulldog clips

Techniques
Basic techniques (see p. 41)
Skiving (see p. 26)
Cutting a strap/belt (see p. 25)
Edge painting (see p. 34)
Bevelling (optional, see p. 33)
Burnishing straps (optional,
    see p. 34)
Saddle stitching (see p. 29)
Attaching a flat magnet (see p. 39)
Attaching a Sam Browne stud
    (see p. 37)

Tote bags are great because they are so roomy, but the downside is that things can get lost in the massive void. This design has an accordion pocket inside that is big enough to hold your wallet, phone and keys.

You will also experiment with weaving, another form of construction. I have chosen to use two contrasting colours of leather as a design choice – you are free to do the same or to keep it all the same colour.

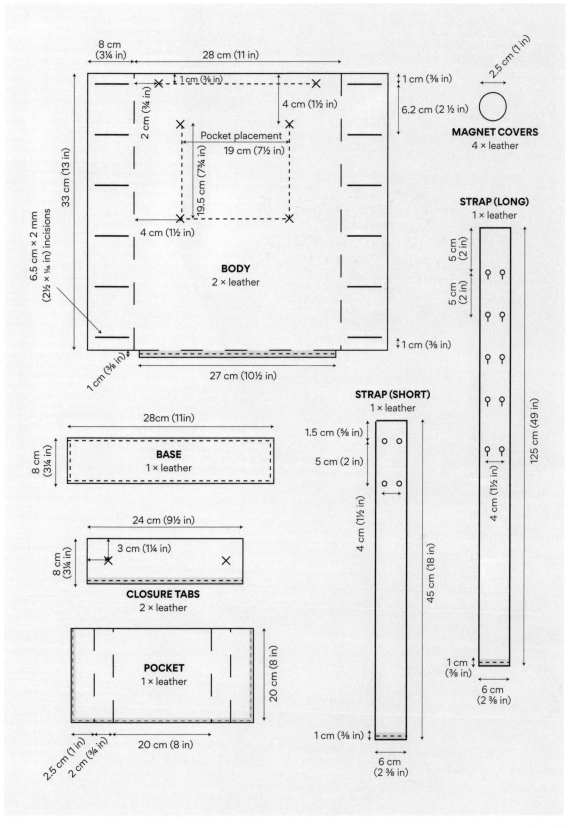

8 cm (3¼ in)

28 cm (11 in)

2.5 cm (1 in)

1 cm (⅜ in)

4 cm (1½ in)

1 cm (⅜ in)

6.2 cm (2 ½ in)

MAGNET COVERS
4 × leather

2 cm (¾ in)

Pocket placement
19 cm (7½ in)

19.5 cm (7¾ in)

4 cm (1½ in)

33 cm (13 in)

6.5 cm × 2 mm
(2½ × ¹⁄₁₆ in) incisions

BODY
2 × leather

1 cm (⅜ in)

STRAP (LONG)
1 × leather

5 cm (2 in)

5 cm (2 in)

1 cm (⅜ in)

1 cm (⅜ in)

27 cm (10½ in)

28cm (11in)

8 cm (3¼ in)

BASE
1 × leather

125 cm (49 in)

4 cm (1½ in)

STRAP (SHORT)
1 × leather

1.5 cm (⅝ in)

5 cm (2 in)

4 cm (1½ in)

24 cm (9½ in)

3 cm (1¼ in)

8 cm (3¼ in)

CLOSURE TABS
2 × leather

45 cm (18 in)

1 cm (⅜ in)

6 cm (2 ⅜ in)

POCKET
1 × leather

20 cm (8 in)

2.5 cm (1 in)

2 cm (¾ in)

20 cm (8 in)

1 cm (⅜ in)

6 cm (2 ⅜ in)

Method

1. Make the pattern and cut the leather

Create the patterns for all pieces apart from the straps. Make the incisions with a knife and the prick marks with an awl. Place the pattern pieces on the grain side of the leather and cut them out. Skive the bottom edges of the body and pocket. For the incisions, use a very sharp knife. Cut the straps using a strap cutter. Cut off the ends to create the correct length before skiving one end of each strap. Measure the holes as indicated on the pattern and hammer them with the 3-mm (⅛-in) hole punch. To make the keyholes, hammer these down with the same hole punch, then make the 5-mm (¼-in) incisions with your knife.

2. Edge paint

Sand around the edges of all the pieces and apply edge paint to all the edges. You can burnish the edges of the straps with a leather palm glove if you prefer. If so, bevel the edges first for a smoother finish – or you can choose to leave the edges angular.

3. Attach the pocket

Fold the pocket at the fold lines so the edges concertina under the central part. Hammer the creases with a palm hammer. Where the folds overlap, use a plastic paddle to apply a 5-mm (¼-in) line of glue along the back of the bottom edge of the pocket, and glue together the innermost folds. Use an awl to scratch the bottom 5 mm of the grain-side edge that will be hidden by the concertina fold. Apply glue to the scratched surface of the grain side and glue these edges together, grain side to grain side. Hammer on top of these folds and glued edges with a palm hammer to set them. Score around the pocket with a divider and around the pocket placement on the body using an awl and metal ruler. Using your pricking chisel, hammer the stitch holes on the grain side for both pieces. Saddle stitch the pocket to the body.

4. Hammer the remaining stitch holes

Using the divider, score a line at the bottom of the closure tab, in between the prick marks at the top and bottom of the body, the bottom of the straps and finally the base. Then use the pricking chisel to hammer down the stitch holes.

- - - - - - - -

5. Attach the magnets

To prepare the closure tabs for attachment to the body, superglue the magnets onto the back of each closure tab. To make sure the magnets face the right way, overlap the closure tabs, grain side to grain side, to ensure that the magnets repel. Wait for the glue to dry before placing a magnet cover over each magnet and scoring around it with the awl. Apply leather glue within this score line and on the back of each magnet cover. Once the glue is tacky, glue the covers down over the magnets.

- - - - - - - -

6. Attach the closure tabs

The closure tabs are pieces that extend from the body pieces. Therefore, they are not to be joined back to back. To attach the first one, place the closure tab grain side up. Then place the body piece over it, also grain side up, aligning the two pieces at the stitch line. The closure tab should extend up from the body. Saddle stitch the closure tab to the body. Repeat with the second closure tab and body piece.

- - - - - - - -

7. Stitch body and straps to base

Hammer down gently with the palm hammer at the folds on both the body pieces. For this project the edges do not need to form one smooth painted edge once stitched, so there is no need to glue the sides together before stitching. Place the first body piece grain side up, then the base piece grain side up over the top, aligning its top stitch line to the bottom stitch line of the body piece. Saddle stitch the base to the body, using a bulldog clip to hold the pieces together at the other end. Then saddle stitch the straps to the short sides of the base.

– – – – – – – –

8. Weave strap to join bag

Once the stitching is complete, the body pieces will come up from the base as the front and back of the bag, and the gussets protruding from the sides of the body will overlap on the sides. For final assembly, align the incisions on the gussets. I have chosen to fold these over so that one painted side of the gusset appears on the front of the bag (the side without the pocket) and the other painted side of the gusset appears on the back. You could have both painted edges facing the same way. Hold the free end of one strap and weave in and out of the incisions until you reach the top. Pull it through until it is taut. Do the same on the other side.

– – – – – – – –

9. Attach the studs

Finally, bring the straps together and make the adjustable strap. On the end of the short strap, there are 4 holes punched to fit the Sam Browne studs. Slot in the screw thread of one stud from the back. Apply a drop of superglue to the screw thread before screwing on the bulb to secure it. Repeat with the other three Sam Browne studs.

Now put the strap together by pushing the studs through the keyholes. Try out the length and make adjustments if you wish. Once adjusted, the tote is ready to be used.

- - - - - - - -

Customization

A great way to customize this project is to create a landscape version by swapping the length and width and turning it into a satchel. Unlike the Shopper, where the top of the bag sits at the elbow, this would sit much lower down, so it would be worth changing the closure to a zip for extra security.

Bumbag/Fanny Pack

Basic leathercraft kit (see p. 41)
Saddle stitch kit (see p. 41)

Materials
Vegetable-tanned leather,
    at least 2 mm (5 oz) thickness
Edge paint
Gum tragacanth
Leather glue
2.5-cm (1-in) buckle
1 turn lock (design of your choice)
Superglue
2 × 6-mm (¼-in) stem standard
    rivets (cap size of your choice)

Tools
Set square
Strap cutter
Beveller
Small brush
Leather-palm glove
8-mm (⁵/₁₆-in) hole punch
3-mm (⅛-in) hole punch
2.5-cm (1-in) long crew punch
Palm hammer
Paring knife
Granite/marble block
Plastic paddle
Small screwdriver (size 2)
Rivet setter

Techniques
Basic techniques (see p. 41)
Cutting a strap/belt (see p. 25)
Edge painting (see p. 34)
Bevelling (see p. 33)
Burnishing (see p. 33)
Skiving (see p. 26)
Saddle stitching (see p. 29)
Setting a standard rivet (see p. 35)

This is a brilliant little bag to keep all your essentials to hand. Offering two looks in one, it can be worn on the shoulder or around the waist.

I've decided to create an angular and structured design for this bag, as opposed to the softer versions you tend to see. Included in this project is a belt, so it is a great way to test what you've learnt from the Belt project.

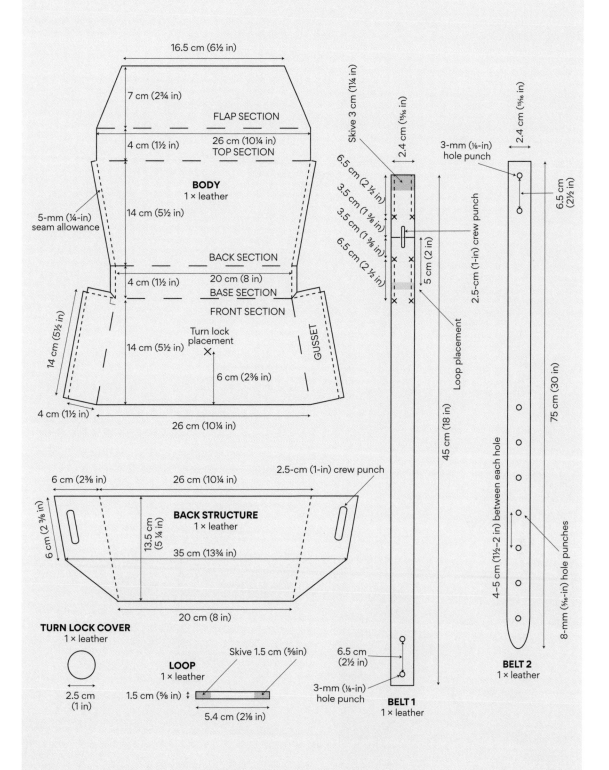

16.5 cm (6½ in)

7 cm (2¾ in)

FLAP SECTION

4 cm (1½ in)   26 cm (10¼ in)
TOP SECTION

BODY
1 × leather

5-mm (¼-in)
seam allowance

14 cm (5½ in)

BACK SECTION

4 cm (1½ in)   20 cm (8 in)
BASE SECTION

14 cm (5½ in)

FRONT SECTION

Turn lock
placement

14 cm (5½ in)

6 cm (2⅜ in)

GUSSET

4 cm (1½ in)

26 cm (10¼ in)

Skive 3 cm (1¼ in)

2.4 cm (⅞ in)

6.5 cm (2½ in)

3.5 cm (1⅜ in)

3.5 cm (1⅜ in)

6.5 cm (2½ in)

Loop placement

2.5-cm (1-in) crew punch

5 cm (2 in)

45 cm (18 in)

3-mm (⅛-in)
hole punch

2.4 cm (⅞ in)

6.5 cm
(2½ in)

75 cm (30 in)

4–5 cm (1½–2 in) between each hole

8-mm (⁵⁄₁₆-in) hole punches

BELT 2
1 × leather

6 cm (2⅜ in)   26 cm (10¼ in)

2.5-cm (1-in) crew punch

6 cm (2 ⅜ in)

BACK STRUCTURE
1 × leather

13.5 cm
(5 ¼ in)

35 cm (13¾ in)

20 cm (8 in)

TURN LOCK COVER
1 × leather

2.5 cm
(1 in)

LOOP
1 × leather

Skive 1.5 cm (⅝in)

1.5 cm (⅝ in)

5.4 cm (2⅛ in)

6.5 cm
(2½ in)

3-mm (⅛-in)
hole punch

BELT 1
1 × leather

Method

- - - - - - - - - - -

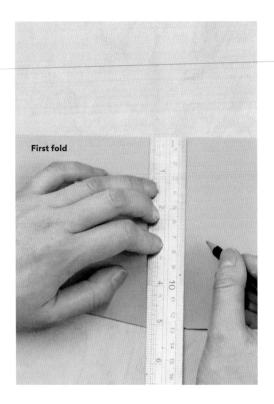

First fold

Front
Base

1. Prepare the pattern

The best way to tackle the diverse widths and angles is to cut the overall lengths first. For the body, make the first fold line and create your perpendicular cut at the base. Measure from this cut edge all the way up, marking the position of each horizontal fold line at the central fold line until you reach 43 cm (16¾ in) from the bottom to top.

The front, base, back, top and flap sections on the body all have different widths. Fold the pattern in half lengthwise and place the metal ruler with 0 cm (0 in) on this centre fold line. Mark half of the overall widths, as indicated on the pattern, at every horizontal fold line. When you open up the fold, this becomes the full width from mark to mark. For example, for the front section, measure 13 cm (5⅛ in) from the fold at the bottom of the pattern, 10 cm (4 in) from the fold for the base section and so forth. Join the dots to complete the sides of the body. The gussets protrude from the sides of the body at 90 degrees to the angled sides. Place your set square base along the side to measure 4 cm (1½ in) outwards at several points. Join the dots to make the gusset edge line. Repeat for the other side. Add a 5-mm (¼-in) seam allowance to the edges, as indicated, before cutting the pattern piece out.

Now use the same method of measuring for the back-structure pattern. Once the pattern is made, draw in the prick marks and fold lines and hammer holes as indicated.

- - - - - - - -

2. Cut the leather

Place the pattern pieces on the grain side of the leather and cut them out. Use a strap cutter set to 2.4 cm (¹⁵⁄₁₆ in) to cut out the belt pieces.

- - - - - - - -

3. Finish the edges and assemble the belt

For the body and back structure, sand down the edges lightly to maintain their sharp, square profile as a stylistic feature. Then apply edge paint with the awl to all the edges of the body and back structure.

For the belt pieces, bevel the edges, sand down to smooth out any fibres, apply gum tragacanth to all sides using a small brush and burnish the edges with the leather-palm glove.

The belt construction is the same as the Belt project (see p. 76), except it is divided into two pieces. Follow the instructions in the Belt project and, using the correct size hole punches, hammer the holes, skive the edges and make the stitch holes using your pricking chisel. Set the buckle (see p. 80) and attach the loop before stitching it together.

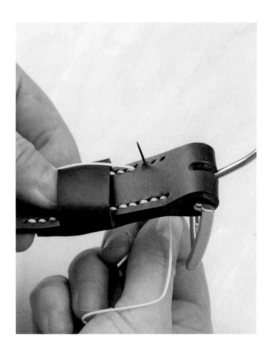

4. Attach the turn lock

Follow the manufacturer's instructions to attach your lock. The lock I have chosen has two prongs to slot in and fold at the back. The closure part has small screws to secure it in place. The best way to judge the placement of your lock is to use the pattern as a prototype and mark in where the lock goes. I centred my lock 6 cm (2 ½ in) down from the opening of the bag. Make a prick mark here to indicate the position. Then mark where the top part of the lock should go on the flap section. Transfer these markings to the leather body. To secure the lock, the two prongs of the lock should go on either side of the marked position. Make 5-mm (¼-in) incisions for the prongs to go through before inserting them, then fold and hammer them down at the back. Cover the back of this by gluing the turn lock cover over it.

Place the top part of the turn lock in position on the flap section. Make prick marks with the awl where you are to screw this in. Cut the slot where the lock would come through by first tracing around it with the awl. With the top of the lock in place, apply a drop of superglue to the screws before screwing them into the leather with a screwdriver.

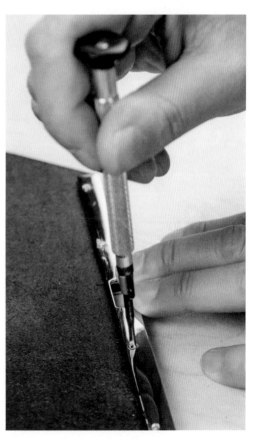

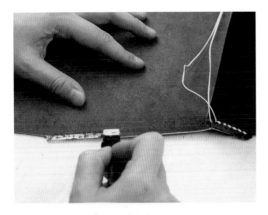

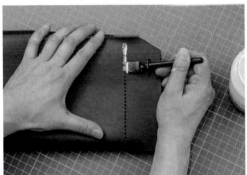

5. Prepare stitch lines and join gusset to base

Fold the leather at the fold lines and hammer down gently with a palm hammer. Score the stitch lines using the divider and hammer down the stitch holes with the pricking chisel on all your pieces.

Apply a thin layer of glue to the back of the stitch line edges that join the base section of the body to the gusset. Once the glue is tacky, glue the stitch sides together and saddle stitch these sections.

Apply a thin layer of glue to the back of the remaining stitch lines on the body. On the back structure piece, you will need to apply a 5-mm (¼-in) strip of glue to both the grain and the back of the stitch line, as this piece is sandwiched between the back section and the gusset sides. Once the glue is tacky, sandwich the back structure between the front and gusset sides. Make sure the stitch holes are completely aligned.

- - - - - - - -

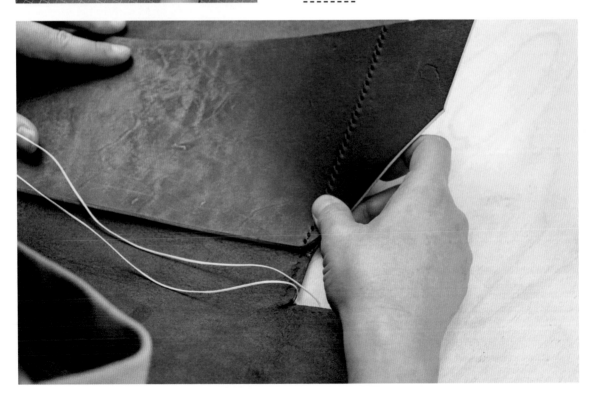

6. Saddle stitch

Measure your stitch length and cut a piece of waxed thread 5–6 times this length to accommodate the thickness of three pieces of leather. Continue stitching from the base section and saddle stitch up towards the flap section. Repeat on the other side to finish constructing the bag.

- - - - - - - -

7. Attach the belt

The final part of construction is to attach the belt to the bag. Using the crew punch, hammer the two holes on the back structure section. There is no need to edge paint or burnish these holes as they will be hidden by the belt. Loop belt 1 through the crew punch hole and secure it with a rivet. Do the same to belt 2 on the other side and again secure it with a rivet. Once this is set, your bag is ready for use.

- - - - - - - -

Customization

Customize by adding extra pockets on the inside, or at the back, to compartmentalize your essentials. By adding slip pockets on the inside, you could essentially turn this into more of a wallet than a bag.

Backpack

Basic leathercraft kit (see p. 41)
Saddle stitching kit (see p. 41)

Materials
Vegetable-tanned leather,
    at least 2 mm (5 oz) thickness
Gum tragacanth
Edge paint
Superglue
5-cm (2-in) length of 1.6-cm (⅝-in)
    wide hook-and-loop tape
16-cm (6¼-in) zip
Leather glue
2 × 2.5-cm (1-in) D-rings
2 × 2.5-cm (1-in) sliders
4 × 6-mm (¼-in) stem standard rivets
    (cap size of your choice)

Tools
Silver pen
Strap cutter
3-mm (⅛-in) hole punch
Paring knife
Granite/marble block
Palm hammer
Beveller
Small brush
Leather-palm glove
Plastic paddle
Lighter
Rivet setter

Techniques
Basic techniques (see p. 41)
Cutting a strap/belt (see p. 25)
Skiving (see p. 26)
Bevelling (see p. 33)
Burnishing straps (see p. 34)
Edge painting (see p. 34)
Tacking (see p. 32)
Saddle stitching (see p. 29)
Setting a standard rivet (see p. 35)

Backpacks are one of my favourite type of bags. They are so versatile, allowing you to go hands-free through your day.

For this project, I have added a small zip pocket to the back to allow easy access to smaller items such as your phone, wallet and keys. This pocket is also hidden when the bag is worn, so it provides that extra bit of security.

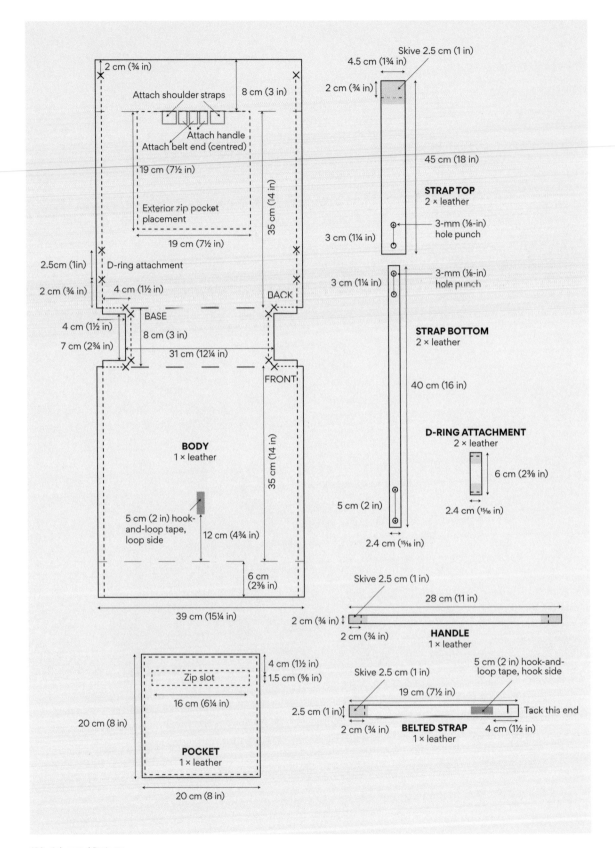

2 cm (¾ in)

8 cm (3 in)

Attach shoulder straps
Attach handle
Attach belt end (centred)

19 cm (7½ in)

Exterior zip pocket placement

35 cm (14 in)

19 cm (7½ in)

2.5cm (1in)

D-ring attachment

2 cm (¾ in)

4 cm (1½ in)

BACK

4 cm (1½ in)

BASE

7 cm (2¾ in)

8 cm (3 in)

31 cm (12¼ in)

FRONT

BODY
1 × leather

35 cm (14 in)

5 cm (2 in) hook-and-loop tape, loop side

12 cm (4¾ in)

6 cm (2⅜ in)

39 cm (15¼ in)

POCKET
1 × leather

Zip slot

4 cm (1½ in)
1.5 cm (⅝ in)

16 cm (6¼ in)

20 cm (8 in)

20 cm (8 in)

Skive 2.5 cm (1 in)

4.5 cm (1¾ in)

2 cm (¾ in)

45 cm (18 in)

STRAP TOP
2 × leather

3 cm (1¼ in)

3-mm (⅛-in) hole punch

3 cm (1¼ in)

3-mm (⅛-in) hole punch

STRAP BOTTOM
2 × leather

40 cm (16 in)

D-RING ATTACHMENT
2 × leather

6 cm (2⅜ in)

2.4 cm (¹⁵⁄₁₆ in)

5 cm (2 in)

2.4 cm (¹⁵⁄₁₆ in)

Skive 2.5 cm (1 in)

28 cm (11 in)

2 cm (¾ in)

2 cm (¾ in)

HANDLE
1 × leather

5 cm (2 in) hook-and-loop tape, hook side

Skive 2.5 cm (1 in)

19 cm (7½ in)

2.5 cm (1 in)

Tack this end

2 cm (¾ in)

BELTED STRAP
1 × leather

4 cm (1½ in)

Method

1. Prepare the pattern and cut the leather

Cut the pocket, body and D-ring attachment pattern pieces. Place these patterns on top of the grain side of the leather and cut around them using a sharp knife. Transfer all the markings to the leather.

Cut the three straps and handle using a strap cutter and punch the holes. Skive 2.5 cm (1 in) from the edges on the handle, belted strap and strap top.

2. Hammer the stitch holes

Score the stitch lines on the grain side of the body and pocket with the divider. Then, using your pricking chisel, hammer down the stitch holes. For the pocket placement on the body, score the stitch lines on the back with an awl and metal ruler before hammering down the stitch holes on the back. You will score and hammer the stitch holes on the handle, belted strap, strap top and D-ring attachment at a later stage.

3. Burnish and edge paint

Bevel the edges of the handle, belted strap, strap top and strap bottom. Using a small brush, apply a layer of gum tragacanth and then burnish these edges using the leather-palm glove. Edge paint all the edges of the pocket and the top edges of the body.

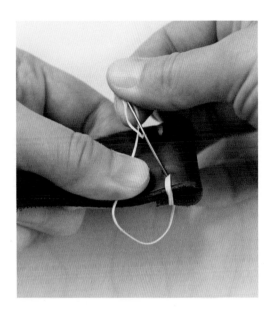

4. Attach the hook-and-loop tape and prepare the belt strap

Apply superglue to the backs of the hook-and-loop tape pieces. Glue down the hook part to the back of the belt strap in the marked position. Glue the loop part to the grain side of the body in the marked position. Scratch the grain side of the glue area on the body first to create a rough surface for better adhesion. Wait for this to dry before continuing.

Tack the end of the belt strap by folding it up approximately 1.5–2 cm (⅝–¾ in). Push a hole through the two pieces approximately 1 cm (⅜ in) from the folded end and 5 mm (¼ in) from the cut edge with the awl. Now tack this end using a needle and waxed thread.

5. Attach the zip to the pocket

First attach the zip. Using a plastic paddle, apply a 5-mm (¼-in) wide strip of leather glue to the back edges of the zip slot. Lay the zip down on the table and place the pocket over it so that the zip fits into the slot perfectly. Saddle stitch around the zip. Once completed, hide the thread ends on the back by cutting them off at the tip, leaving approximately 2 mm (¹⁄₁₆ in). Melt the thread ends with a lighter.

6. Attach straps to the top of the pocket

The handle, belt strap and strap top are aligned at the top of the pocket and stitched down. On the grain side of the skived ends of these pieces, use an awl to scratch the surface 2 cm (¾ in) from the end; the rough surface will stick to the back of the pocket more easily.

Apply a thin layer of leather glue to the top of the pocket. Then apply leather glue 2 cm (¾ in) from the edge to the scratched grain surfaces of the handle and belt strap, and the back of the strap top.

Once the glue is tacky, stick the belt strap down at the top centre of the pocket. Lay the pocket grain side up on the hammering block, with the belt strap glued at the top. Take the pricking chisel and hammer over the previously made stitch holes to extend them through the glued-down belt strap.

Turn the pocket over and glue the grain side of the handle ends to the back of the pocket, either side of the belt strap. Glue the back of the strap tops to the back of the pocket on either side of the handle. Hammer these down lightly with the palm hammer to set them in place and wait until the glue is dry. Extend the stitch holes through the elements you have added at the top, as you did for the strap.

- - - - - - - -

7. Attach the pocket to the body

Place the pocket in position over the body and align it so that the stitch holes match up. Saddle stitch around it to secure it to the body. Once completed, you can hide the thread ends on the back. Cut off, leaving 2 mm (1⁄16 in), and melt the ends with a lighter.

- - - - - - - -

8. Attach the D-ring attachment

Pull the D-ring attachment through the D-ring and fold the leather in half. Apply a small amount of leather glue to the skived ends and glue them together once the glue is tacky. Take the awl and scratch the grain sides of the skived part. Repeat for the second D-ring. Apply leather glue to one side of each D-ring attachment and glue them in position in between the prick marks on the back of the body. Hammer gently with a palm hammer and wait for the glue to dry.

- - - - - - - -

Place the body on a hammering block, grain side up. Use the pricking chisel to extend the stitch holes through the D-ring attachments.

- - - - - - - -

9. Saddle stitch the sides

Apply a 5-mm (¼-in) wide strip of leather glue along the back of the stitch edges of the body. Once the glue is tacky, glue the sides together, making sure the edges are flush to form the final T-shaped base of the bag. Saddle stitch the sides together.

- - - - - - - -

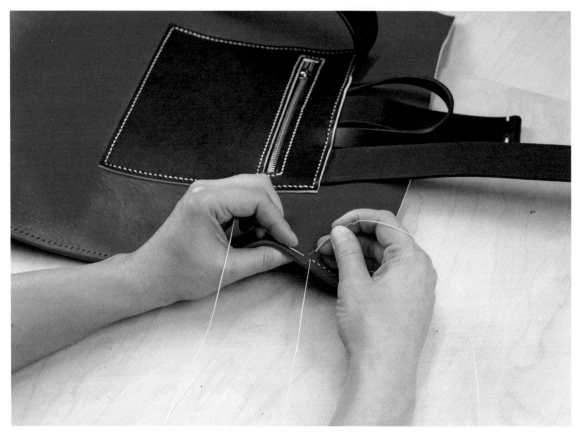

10. Attach the strap bottom

Take the strap bottom and loop it around the centre bar of the slider. Allow the two holes to meet and put a rivet through this to secure it. Set the rivet.

Bring the other end of the strap bottom through the D-ring, then back through the two sides of the slider. Bring the strap bottom up to meet the strap top and secure them together with rivets. Repeat for the other side, and your backpack is ready to use.

- - - - - - - -

Customization

This backpack is a reiteration of the T-based construction from the Wristlet project (see p. 88) – a perfect example of how different shapes can be changed and accessorized to create an entirely new bag. While I like a clean and minimalist design, another way to customize this bag is to add extra pockets to the front, securing the opening with hook-and-loop tape or a zip.

Handbag/Purse

Basic leathercraft kit (see p. 41)
Saddle stitching kit (see p. 41)

Materials
Vegetable-tanned leather,
    at least 2 mm (5 oz) thickness
Edge paint
Superglue
Leather glue
4 × 1.5-cm (⅝-in) diameter
    flat magnets
2 × 8-mm (⁵/₁₆-in) wide cap,
    screw-on rivets (you can use
    normal rivets if you wish)

Tools
Compass
Silver pen
Paring knife
Granite/marble block
5-mm (¼-in) hole punch
2 or 3 prong pricking chisel,
    3-mm (⅛-in) stitch length
Palm hammer
2–4 bulldog clips
Small piece of cork

Techniques
Basic techniques (see p. 41)
Cutting rounded corners
    (see p. 24)
Skiving (see p. 26)
Edge painting (see p. 34)
Attaching a flat magnet (see p. 39)
Saddle stitching (see p. 29)
Setting a screw-on rivet (see p. 36)

In this project you will try your hand at creating a rounded bag, and you'll learn how to setting a gusset that fits into a rounded shape.

You will also learn another method of saddle stitching that uses the awl to create the hole for each stitch. For the wrist strap I have used a 5-mm (¼-in) hole punch for the rivet attachment, as I want the wrist strap to be able to swing. However, if you wish for it to be fixed, you can use a 3-mm (⅛-in) hole punch.

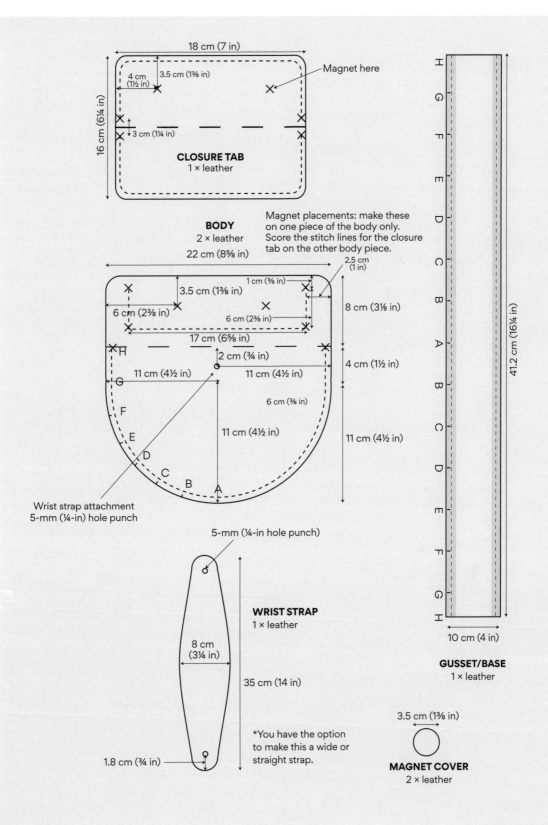

18 cm (7 in)

4 cm (1½ in)   3.5 cm (1⅜ in)

Magnet here

16 cm (6¼ in)

3 cm (1¼ in)

CLOSURE TAB
1 × leather

BODY
2 × leather

22 cm (8⅝ in)

Magnet placements: make these on one piece of the body only. Score the stitch lines for the closure tab on the other body piece.

2.5 cm (1 in)

1 cm (⅜ in)

3.5 cm (1⅜ in)

6 cm (2⅜ in)

6 cm (2⅜ in)

8 cm (3⅛ in)

17 cm (6⅝ in)

4 cm (1½ in)

2 cm (¾ in)

H

11 cm (4½ in)   11 cm (4½ in)

G

6 cm (⅜ in)

F

E

11 cm (4½ in)

11 cm (4½ in)

D

C

B

A

Wrist strap attachment
5-mm (¼-in) hole punch

5-mm (¼-in hole punch)

WRIST STRAP
1 × leather

8 cm (3¼ in)

35 cm (14 in)

1.8 cm (¾ in)

*You have the option to make this a wide or straight strap.

H
G
F
E
D
C
B
A
B
C
D
E
F
G
H

41.2 cm (16¼ in)

10 cm (4 in)

GUSSET/BASE
1 × leather

3.5 cm (1⅜ in)

MAGNET COVER
2 × leather

Method

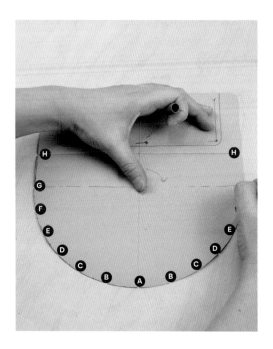

1. Prepare the body pattern

Create the body pattern piece. It is best to use a compass for the semi-circular front. Make sure the fold of this pattern is at the centre so that, when it is opened, the sides perfectly mirror each other. Label this the first fold. Keep the pattern folded and label the bottom of the fold at the round edge A. From here, make notches roughly 3 cm (1¼ in) apart until you reach the straight edge at H. Write in A, B, C, D, E, etc. along these notches, starting with A at the base of the fold. You can make the 3-cm (1¼-in) approximation by eye, as you will transfer these notches from the rounded edge to a straight edge on the gusset/base so that, when you glue the leather pieces together, they will match. Unfold the pattern and transfer the notches to the other side and mirror the labels. Draw in a 5-mm (¼-in) seam allowance along the rounded edge of the body. Draw in a stitch line 5 mm (¼ in) within the rounded cut edge of the body from H to H.

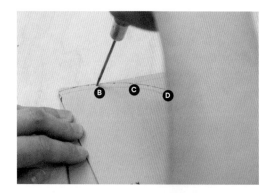

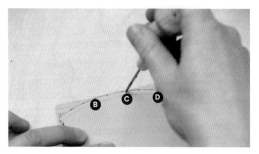

2. Prepare the remaining pattern pieces

Cut a piece of pattern paper approximately 55 cm (22 in) long (longer than the gusset length) at the correct width of 10 cm (4 in). Draw in the 5-mm (¼-in) seam allowance on the long edges. Fold the gusset in half so you are working with half the length and label this the first fold. Mark the corner A. Lay the gusset down on the cutting mat. Now place the body over the top, so that the first fold of both pieces is aligned at A. Take the awl and follow along the drawn-in stitch line until you reach B, gently moving the curved edge so that it swivels along the straight edge. Make sure the edges of the gusset and body remain flush. Press down with the awl at B to prick mark the position. Continue this way to C, D, etc until you reach the prick mark H. You have reached the edge of the gusset where the stitching stops. Remove the body from the gusset. Your prick marks will have gone through two layers of pattern paper on the gusset, mirroring each other. Keep the gusset folded and cut across at H, then open the pattern up and label the rest of the prick marks.

3. Cut the leather

Once all the pattern pieces are made, cut the leather and transfer the pattern markings. When you transfer the markings to the body leather, make sure that the stitch line for the closure tab goes on one piece of the body and the magnet placement on the other piece. For the curved shapes, score around the pattern with an awl before cutting. Skive the long edges of the gusset.

Once all the pieces are cut, mark the notches on the body and gusset by making a deep mark with the awl on the back, but do not go all the way through to the grain side. The notches only need to be visible on the back. You could transfer the letters across with a silver pen to remind yourself of their position. Transfer all remaining prick marks and punch out the holes on the wrist strap and body.

- - - - - - - -

4. Edge paint

Sand down the edges of the leather pieces. This is a chance to clean up any messy cut edges and make them smooth. Apply edge paint to all the non-stitch edges of the body and gusset, and the entirety of the wrist strap and closure tab.

- - - - - - - -

5. Attach the magnets

To attach the magnets to the opening of the bag, glue them down with superglue on the back of one of the body pieces and on the back of the closure tab. Ensure that you glue the magnets down on the correct side so that, when they come together, they attract.

Once the glue has dried, place one of the magnet covers over a magnet on the back of the body piece and score around it. Apply leather glue within the score line and to the back of the magnet cover and stick together once the glue is tacky. Repeat with the second magnet cover and body magnet.

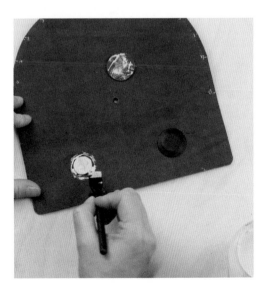

- - - - - - - -

6. Hammer the stitch holes

Score in the lines for saddle stitching for all the pieces using the divider. Then, using the pricking chisel, hammer down the holes on the closure tab and body. For the closure tab stitch line on the body, use a metal ruler and awl to score from prick mark to prick mark. Do not hammer the stitch holes on the gusset.

- - - - - - - -

7. Attach the closure tab

Fold the closure tab as indicated and hammer down gently with a palm hammer to reinforce the fold. Sandwich this around the top of the second body piece, aligning it with the stitch holes you have already made. Take note that this is not the body piece to which you have attached the magnets. You can glue the pieces together before saddle stitching or clip the edges with bulldog clips. Measure the stitch line and cut 5–6 times this length of waxed thread, as we are stitching through three pieces of leather. Saddle stitch these pieces together.

- - - - - - - -

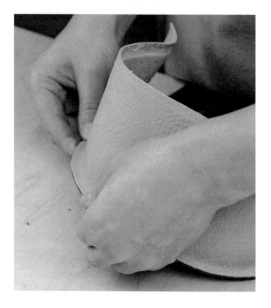

8. Glue the gusset in place

Apply a small layer of glue on the back of the stitch edge of one body piece and one long edge of the gusset. Once the glue is tacky, start at A on both pieces and press together. Then press the pieces together at H before matching the letters in between at B, C, D, etc. By starting at A and H, you will be able to manipulate the leather to fit within the curve. Once completed, glue down the other side.

- - - - - - - -

9. Saddle stitch gusset to body

Rest the cork on the edge of the table and lay the seam edge of the body and gusset on top, with the prick marks uppermost. Take the awl and pierce through each stitch hole from the grain side of the body through the gusset and into the cork. Once all the holes are made, saddle stitch the body to the gusset. Once stitched, sand down these edges and apply edge paint using the awl.

- - - - - - - -

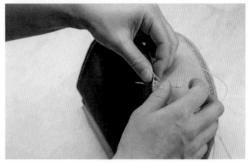

10. Attach the wrist strap

To complete the bag, reach inside the bag with the stem part of the screw-on rivet and push it through the hole. Place the hole of one end of the wrist strap over this stem. Add a small amount of superglue to the stem part and twist on the top of the rivet. Attach the other end of the wrist strap in the same way. Your handbag is now complete.

- - - - - - - -

Customization

The easiest way to customize this bag is to change the handle to a strap and make it into a crossbody bag.
If you are up for a challenge, you can make the bag smaller or bigger by adjusting the front and back pieces.
It could then work as a mini coin purse or a large tote.

Bucket Bag

Basic leathercraft kit (see p. 41)
Saddle stitching kit (see p. 41)

Materials
Vegetable-tanned leather, at
    least 2 mm (5 oz) thickness
    (choose a soft leather so that
    you can turn it easily once
    stitched together)
Vegetable-tanned leather, at
    least 3 mm (7½ oz) thickness
    for the straps and drawstring
    tab (choose a stiffer leather
    for this)
Gum tragacanth
Leather glue

Tools
Compass or a large round object
    with the correct circumference
Silver pen
Paring knife
Granite/marble block
Strap cutter
Beveller
Leather-palm glove
Pricking chisel,
    3-mm (⅛-in) stitch length
Plastic paddle
Roller
6–8 small bulldog clips
Small rectangular piece of cork
1.5-cm (⅝-in) hole punch

Techniques
Basic techniques (see p. 41)
Cutting a strap/belt (see p. 25)
Skiving (see p. 26)
Bevelling (see p. 33)
Burnishing straps (see p. 34)
Saddle stitching (see p. 29)

The bucket bag is a wonderful design to add to your collection. The key to creating a neat and perfect finish is all in the pattern making.

This is the first and only bag in this book where you'll learn how to create a bag where the stitching is hidden inside. I often choose to machine stitch this type of bag, as the beauty of hand stitching should be shown off on the outside. However, it is good to understand how this type of construction is done even when hiding your hand stitching.

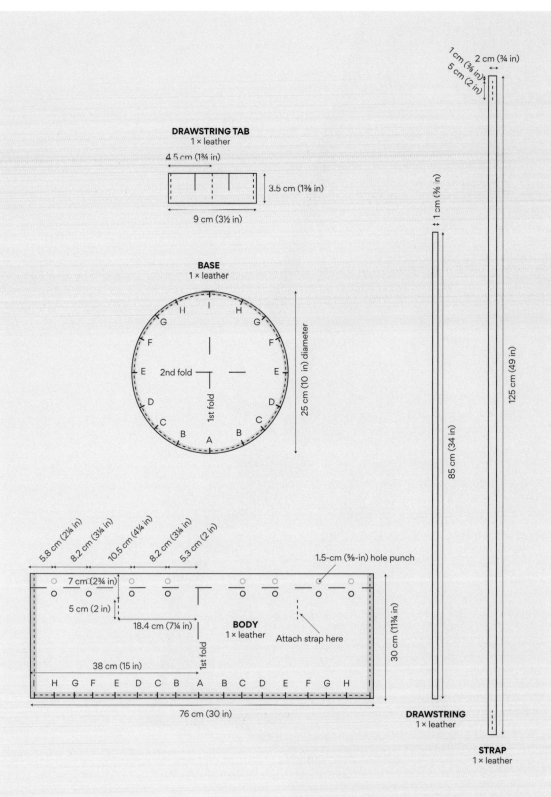

DRAWSTRING TAB
1 × leather

4.5 cm (1¾ in)

3.5 cm (1⅜ in)

9 cm (3½ in)

BASE
1 × leather

G H I H G
F F
E 2nd fold E
1st fold
D D
C B A B C

25 cm (10 in) diameter

2 cm (¾ in)
1 cm (⅜ in)
5 cm (2 in)

1 cm (⅜ in)

125 cm (49 in)

85 cm (34 in)

5.8 cm (2¼ in) 8.2 cm (3¼ in) 10.5 cm (4¼ in) 8.2 cm (3¼ in) 5.3 cm (2 in)

1.5-cm (⅝-in) hole punch

7 cm (2¾ in)

5 cm (2 in)

18.4 cm (7¼ in)

BODY
1 × leather

Attach strap here

1st fold

30 cm (11¾ in)

38 cm (15 in)

H G F E D C B A B C D E F G H

76 cm (30 in)

DRAWSTRING
1 × leather

STRAP
1 × leather

Method

1. Prepare the base pattern

Draw and cut out the base circle before folding it into quarters to get a perpendicular fold. Call the vertical fold the first fold and the horizontal fold the second fold.

Create notches at the ends of the perpendicular fold labelled A and I, and at the ends of the horizontal fold labelled E. Now refold the pattern on the first fold and create three notches in between A and E, and three notches in between E and I. These notches do not need to be exact points on the curve. They will work as a guide for you when you attach it to the body. Open the pattern up and mark it alphabetically.

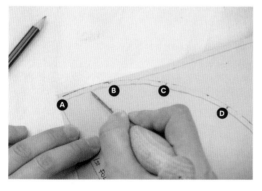

2. Prepare the body and drawstring tab patterns

Measure a pattern piece for the body 30 cm (11¾ in) wide as marked on the pattern, but longer than marked – roughly 90 cm (35 in). Fold it in half lengthwise and call this the first fold. At the base of this fold, make a notch and call it A. Draw in the stitch lines, leaving 5 mm (¼ in) for the seam.

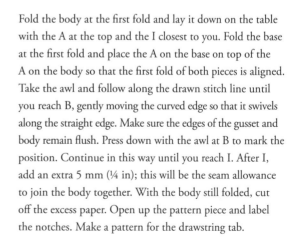

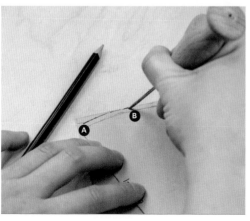

Fold the body at the first fold and lay it down on the table with the A at the top and the I closest to you. Fold the base at the first fold and place the A on the base on top of the A on the body so that the first fold of both pieces is aligned. Take the awl and follow along the drawn stitch line until you reach B, gently moving the curved edge so that it swivels along the straight edge. Make sure the edges of the gusset and body remain flush. Press down with the awl at B to mark the position. Continue in this way until you reach I. After I, add an extra 5 mm (¼ in); this will be the seam allowance to join the body together. With the body still folded, cut off the excess paper. Open up the pattern piece and label the notches. Make a pattern for the drawstring tab.

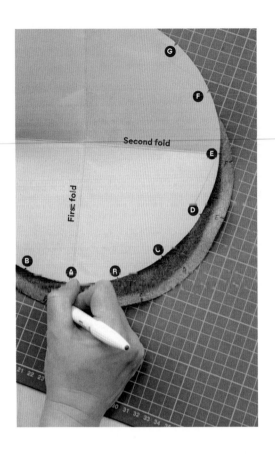

Second fold

First fold

G
F
E
D
C
B
A
R

3. Cut the leather

Place the body and base pattern pieces on top of the grain side of the leather and cut them out. Score around the circular base to make it easier to cut without the hindrance of the pattern on top.

Skive the edges of the base and body with a paring knife. Practise skiving a rounded edge on a scrap piece first before skiving the base. Skive approximately 2.5 cm (1 in) at a time and sharpen your paring knife as soon as you feel it is blunt. On the back of these pieces, mark the notches but do not press the awl all the way through to the grain side. You want the points to be just deep enough for you to see. Label them A to I. Using an awl, mark the position of the holes where the drawstring will go through on the grain side.

Cut the strap and drawstring with a strap cutter. For the drawstring tab, place the pattern piece on top of the grain side of the leather and cut it out. Bevel the edges and burnish the strap, drawstring and the drawstring tab using a leather-palm glove.

4. Hammer the stitch holes and join the body

Use a divider to score in the stitch lines on the edges of the body and drawstring tab. With an awl and metal ruler, score the two lines for the strap attachment on the body, the stitch lines on the strap and the stitch line in the centre of the drawstring tab. Hammer down the stitch holes along the score lines. Do not make stitch holes in the base.

Saddle stitch the body together to create a cylindrical shape. As you will turn the bag inside out later, match the edges of the grain sides together and saddle stitch. To glue down the seam, apply glue to the edges and use a roller to open the seam out like a butterfly.

----

5. Reinforce the opening of the bag

Fold the top of the bag "cylinder" over by 2.5 cm (1 in).
Run a roller over this fold. Open it out again and apply
leather glue to the top 5 cm (2 in) at the back of the
cylindrical body, and, once the glue is tacky, fold down
again at 2.5 cm (1 in) and secure by running a roller over it.

- - - - - - - -

6. Glue the base

Apply a thin layer of glue to the grain side of the stitch edge
of the body and base. Once the glue is tacky, attach A on the
body to the A on the base, E to E and I to I, making sure
the edges are flush. Use small bulldog clips to help keep the
pieces in the correct position. Stretch out the leather to fill
in the gaps to fit around the base, using extra bulldog clips
to hold the body and base together along the glued edges.

- - - - - - - -

7. Transfer stitch holes and saddle stitch the base

Place the small piece of cork on the edge of the table and lay the seam edge on it, with the body on top. Using the awl, punch through each stitch hole so that it pierces through the base and the cork. Measure the circumference of the base and cut 4–5 times the length of waxed thread. Saddle stitch the body and base together. Once completed, turn inside out to reveal the bucket bag shape.

8. Punch holes for the drawstring

Following the measurements on the body pattern, use the 1.5-cm (⅝-in) hole punch punch to make the the holes for the drawstring in the positions you have marked. The best way to do this is to slide your hammering block into the bag before hammering the holes with the hole punch.

----

9. Attach the drawstring

Assemble the drawstring tab by folding the short edges over so that they overlap in the centre. Take approximately 25 cm (10 in) of waxed thread and saddle stitch this together so that you have two cylindrical holes on either side of the stitch line. Pull the drawstring through one side of the drawstring tab and then through the 1.5-cm (⅝-in) holes on the top of the body, weaving it in and out of the holes. Once the drawstring reaches the front, pull the end through the second hole on the drawstring tab. Tie a knot at each end.

10. Attach the strap

To attach the strap, take approximately 25 cm (10 in) of waxed thread and saddle stitch the end of the strap to the side of the bag. Do the same to the other side to complete.

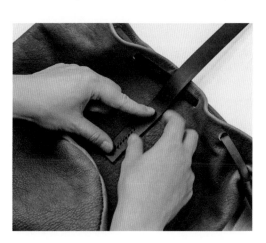

Customization

One of my favourite ways to customize this bag is to make a large version and turn it into a duffle bag.
It will be the perfect size as an overnight bag with an added over-the-shoulder strap.
You can also create pockets inside for your toiletries and other essentials.

Taking it Further

Creating Your Own Leather Designs

The aim of this chapter is to demonstrate how you can take the techniques and constructions learned in the previous projects and adapt them to create completely different designs.

I began my own leathercraft journey by learning essential leatherworking skills and then designing and making products in basic shapes similar to the Passport Holder and Wristlet. The advent of the real fun for me was when I began to experiment with different designs and features. No doubt I was inspired by the many bag designs out there. If you look closely at them, you will see that they are made with just a few basic methods. The projects in this book have introduced you to some of these: the T-base in the Backpack and Wristlet projects, the inset gusset of the Toiletry Bag, the gusset and base of the Handbag/Purse, the construction of the Bucket Bag, and the hidden gusset on the Crossbody Bag. All of these basic construction styles can be adapted to create different bags.

Before you jump straight into designing your own collection, there are a few crucial design aspects to consider. First is the notion that "form follows function". This phrase was coined by architect Louis Sullivan, and the idea was a principle of twentieth-century minimalist architecture and industrial design. Functionality outweighs design such that you cannot have a laptop bag that does not fit a laptop or a cardholder where the slots are too large and the cards fall out.

Second to functionality is ergonomics. As bags and accessories are wearable objects, they must fit around the body comfortably. For example, if a large tote bag is supported by thin straps, these will eventually cut into the shoulder when the bag is loaded with heavy objects. I have always believed that good design comes out of understanding the constraints.

I am now going to take you through three projects to show you the possibilities and potential of using all the skills you have learned in the previous chapters. The projects here are are arranged in order of difficulty, with the simplest first.

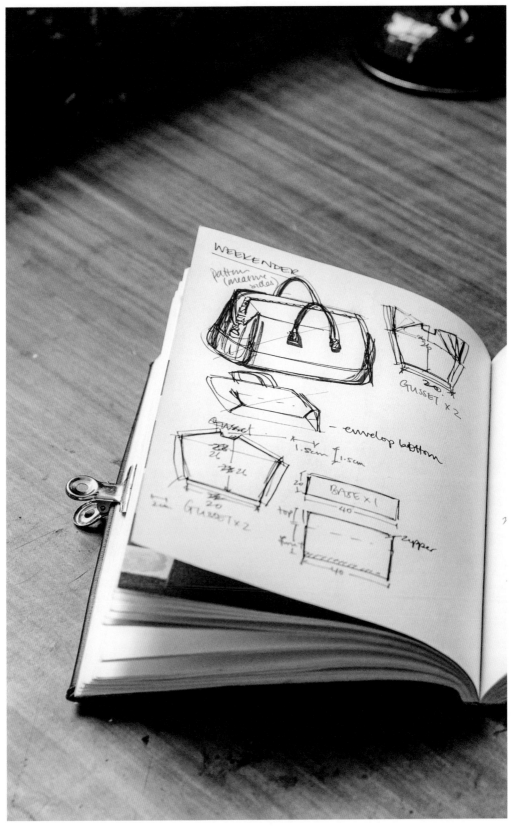

Plant Holder

Basic leathercraft kit (see p. 41)

Materials
Vegetable-tanned leather,
    at least 2 mm (5 oz) thickness
    (choose a stiff leather so the
    holder maintains its shape)
Gum tragacanth
2 × 7-mm (¼-in) stem
    standard rivets

Tools
Strap cutter
3-mm (⅛-in) hole punch
Palm hammer
Beveller
Burnisher
Leather-palm glove
Rivet setter

Techniques
Basic techniques (see p. 41)
Cutting a strap/belt (see p. 25)
Bevelling (see p. 33)
Burnishing (see p. 33)
Burnishing straps (see p. 34)
Setting a standard rivet (see p. 35)

The plant holder is an iteration of the Keychain Lanyard (see p. 66). We are not simply resizing this object, but creating an entirely new product.

This design is essentially an upside-down version of the lanyard with the dimensions extended to fit the potted plant of your choice. This customization project is about challenging you with pattern making. You may also choose to not create a strap if you intend to place the plant holder on a table instead of hanging it.

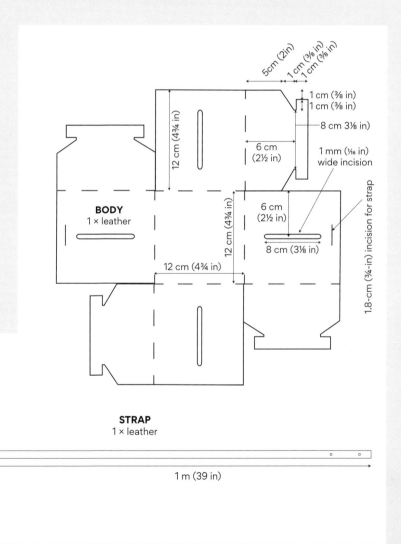

5cm (2in)
1 cm (⅜ in)
1 cm (⅜ in)
1 cm (⅜ in)
1 cm (⅜ in)
8 cm 3⅛ in)
1 mm (1/16 in) wide incision
12 cm (4¾ in)
6 cm (2½ in)
6 cm (2½ in)
12 cm (4¾ in)
8 cm (3⅛ in)
12 cm (4¾ in)
1.8-cm (¾-in) incision for strap

BODY
1 × leather

STRAP
1 × leather

3-mm (⅛-in) hole punch
6 mm (¼ in)
9 mm (⅜ in)
4 cm (1 in)
1 m (39 in)

Method

1. Cut the pattern and leather

I have made a plant holder with a 12 × 12-cm (4¾ × 4¾-in) base that is 12 cm (4¾ in) high. Change the measurements on the pattern depending on how big you want your plant holder to be. Draw out the base first on the body pattern, using the first and second folds of basic pattern making to get an accurate square. Measure out the sides from here. Draw the folding flaps as extensions from the sides. Starting with the side at the top, extend from its right side and measure 5 cm (2 in), then 1 cm (⅜ in), and another 1 cm (⅜ in). Following the pattern, draw in and cut out the indents to create the shape. Use the same technique for the remaining flaps. Make all the incisions on the pattern before placing it on the grain side of the leather and cutting out. Use a strap cutter to make the strap. Punch the holes and make the incisions on both leather pieces.

- - - - - - - -

2. Bevel and burnish the edges

Bevel all the external edges of the body and the strap. Leave the other cut edges of the body, as they will be hidden once the plant holder is assembled. Apply gum tragacanth and burnish the edges of the body with a burnisher. Burnish the edges of the strap using a leather-palm glove.

- - - - - - - -

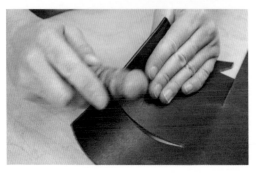

3. Assemble the plant holder

Before assembling, press down on the folds and hammer them down lightly with a palm hammer. This will help to create the box shape. You could skip this step if you want the end result to be more rounded. Connect all the sides by slotting the ends of the flaps into the slots.

- - - - - - - -

4. Attach the strap

To attach the strap, slot one end into the incision from the grain side. Pull it through and allow the holes to meet. Secure the strap with a rivet. To complete the plant holder, attach the other end of the strap using the same method.

- - - - - - - -

Box Handbag/Purse with Fringe

- -

Basic leathercraft kit (see p. 41)
Saddle stitching kit (see p. 41)

Materials
Vegetable-tanned leather,
    at least 2 mm (5 oz) thickness
    in two colours (or stick with
    one colour if you prefer)
Edge paint
Leather glue

Tools
Paring knife
Granite/marble block
Palm hammer
Plastic paddle
8 extra harness needles (optional)

Techniques
Basic techniques (see p. 41)
Skiving (see p. 26)
Edge painting (see p. 34)
Gluing (see p. 28)
Saddle stitching (see p. 29)

This is an iteration of the Crossbody Bag and Tote projects (see p. 112 and 120), using the same hidden gussets and the weave as a decorative element.

I have added decorative elements to this bag to give you an idea of how you can transform a relatively simple box shape to something even more dynamic.

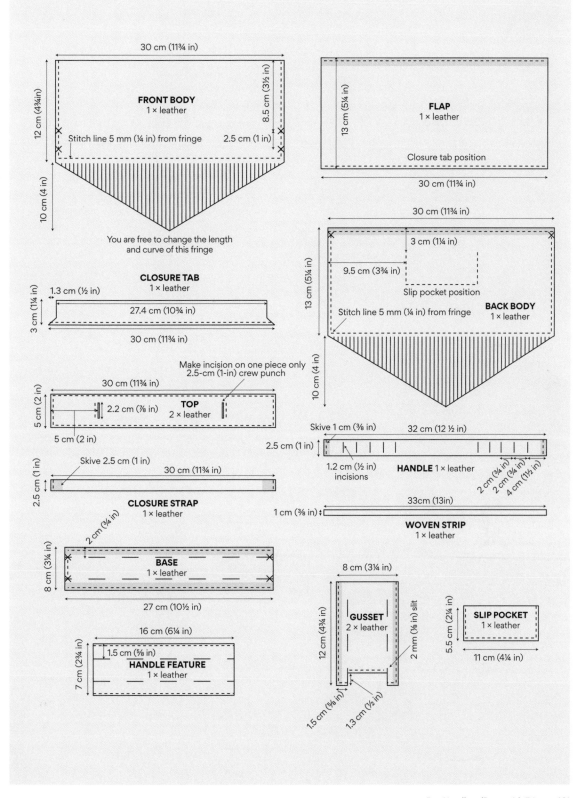

FRONT BODY
1 × leather

30 cm (11¾ in)

12 cm (4¾in)

8.5 cm (3½ in)

Stitch line 5 mm (¼ in) from fringe

2.5 cm (1 in)

10 cm (4 in)

You are free to change the length
and curve of this fringe

FLAP
1 × leather

13 cm (5¼ in)

Closure tab position

30 cm (11¾ in)

CLOSURE TAB
1 × leather

1.3 cm (½ in)

3 cm (1¼ in)

27.4 cm (10¾ in)

30 cm (11¾ in)

30 cm (11¾ in)

3 cm (1¼ in)

9.5 cm (3¾ in)

Slip pocket position

13 cm (5¼ in)

BACK BODY
1 × leather

Stitch line 5 mm (¼ in) from fringe

10 cm (4 in)

Make incision on one piece only
2.5-cm (1-in) crew punch

30 cm (11¾ in)

5 cm (2 in)

2.2 cm (⅞ in)

TOP
2 × leather

5 cm (2 in)

Skive 1 cm (⅜ in)

32 cm (12 ½ in)

2.5 cm (1 in)

1.2 cm (½ in)
incisions

HANDLE 1 × leather

2 cm (¾ in) 2 cm (¾ in)
4 cm (1½ in)

Skive 2.5 cm (1 in)

2.5 cm (1 in)

30 cm (11¾ in)

CLOSURE STRAP
1 × leather

33cm (13in)

1 cm (⅜ in)

WOVEN STRIP
1 × leather

2 cm (¾ in)

8 cm (3¼ in)

BASE
1 × leather

27 cm (10½ in)

16 cm (6¼ in)

7 cm (2¾ in)

1.5 cm (⅝ in)

HANDLE FEATURE
1 × leather

8 cm (3¼ in)

12 cm (4¾ in)

GUSSET
2 × leather

2 mm (⅛ in) slit

1.5 cm (⅝ in) 1.3 cm (½ in)

5.5 cm (2¼ in)

SLIP POCKET
1 × leather

11 cm (4¼ in)

Method

1. Prepare the pattern and cut the leather

Create and cut out the pattern pieces, labelling each one carefully. For the front body and back body patterns, cut the overall rectangle size first. Draw in the fringe shape, either as shown here or of your own design. The width of each fringe piece is 1 cm (⅜ in). Mark the 1-cm (⅜-in) increments with an awl at the top and bottom of the fringe section. Place the metal ruler on the pattern, aligning the top and bottom marks to create a vertical line. Once the pattern pieces are cut and the prick marks pencilled in, place them on the grain side and cut the leather pieces. Transfer the markings and skive the edges where indicated. Cut the incisions for the handle through both the pattern paper and the leather.

2. Hammer the stitch holes

Score in the stitch lines on the leather with a divider. In places where the stitch line is not on the edge of the leather, use the awl and metal ruler to do this. Hammer down the stitch holes.

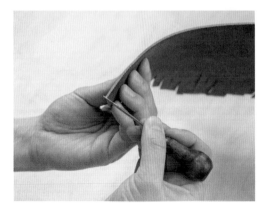

3. Edge paint
Edge paint the top of the front body, the sides of the flap, the top of the gussets, the top and sides of the closure tab, all edges of the top, the long sides of the closure strap, the top of the slip pocket, the sides of the handle and woven strip, and all sides of the handle feature. Edge painting the fringe runs the risk of spreading the paint across the leather. I suggest you paint just the outer edge and leave the fringe with a raw edge.

4. Attach the slip pocket

Apply a 5-mm (¼-in) wide strip of leather glue along the back of the stitch line of the pocket on the back of the back body and slip pocket. Glue down once tacky, ensuring that the stitch holes match up. Saddle stitch together.

- - - - - - - -

5. Assemble the handle

Weave the woven strip piece in and out of the incisions made on the handle. Insert the woven strip piece into the handle from the back to begin weaving. This weave is a design feature and it also strengthens the handle. Slot each end of the handle through the 2.2-cm (⅞-in) incisions of the top piece from the grain side. Pull the handle 1 cm (⅜ in) into the incision, place it over a hammering block and place the pricking chisel over the already punched holes on the top piece. Hammer through all three pieces of leather and saddle stitch them together on both sides.

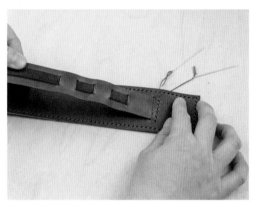

- - - - - - - -

6. Attach the closure strap to the front, and attach the closure tab to the flap

Apply a small amount of glue to the stitch edge in between the prick marks on the front body. Scratch the leather with an awl on the grain side of the front body to help the glue to adhere. Once the glue is tacky, stick the closure strap down. To attach the closure tab, apply a layer of glue 5 mm (¼ in) wide to the stitch edge of the closure tab and the bottom of the flap.

To attach the closure tab to the flap, apply a line of glue 5 mm (¼ in) wide to the stitch edges of the closure tab and the bottom of the flap. Once tacky, glue and saddle stitch these pieces together.

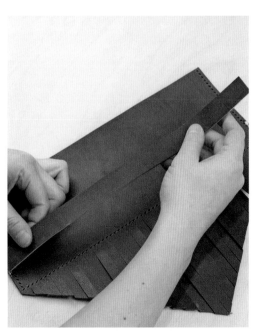

- - - - - - - -

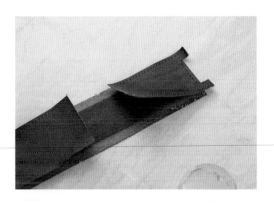

7. Attach the gussets to the base

Fold the gusset edges towards the grain side as indicated on the pattern, press down and hammer gently with a palm hammer to reinforce the folds. Align one side of the base with the bottom edge of the gusset. Apply a thin layer of leather glue to the back of both pieces on the stitch lines and press them together once tacky. Saddle stitch. Repeat on the other side.

- - - - - - - -

8. Assemble the bag exterior

The bag is constructed by attaching the flap and back body pieces to the top section. Apply leather glue to the back of the top stitch edge of the flap, the top and bottom stitch edges of the top (the piece without the handle) and the top stitch edge of the back body. Glue them together, making sure that all the stitch holes are aligned.

To attach the handle to the top of the bag, scratch with the awl on the top edge of the grain sides of the flap and back body piece about 5 mm (¼ in) from the edge. Apply a thin layer of glue to these edges as well as all around the stitch line on the back of the top piece with the handle. Once the glue is tacky, press down, making sure the stitch holes are aligned. Saddle stitch the two top pieces to the flap and back body to complete the bag exterior.

- - - - - - - -

9. Assemble the bag

Before attaching the final pieces, reinforce the folds of the gussets and base using the palm hammer. Glue the front body to the already assembled gusset and base by applying glue to the remaining stitch lines and then saddle stitching them together. When gluing, I place spare needles through some of the holes just above the fringe to make sure that the stitch holes are aligned on the front body and base.

Attach the back body to the gusset and base and stitch them together. Sand down all the raw edges with sandpaper and apply edge paint with the awl. Apply paint to one side first and allow the edges to dry before tackling the other side, to ensure that no paint smudges the surface on your bag.

- - - - - - - -

10. Attach the handle feature

To complete the bag, attach the handle feature, which reinforces the handle. Wrap the piece around the handle and saddle stitch across the top.

- - - - - - - -

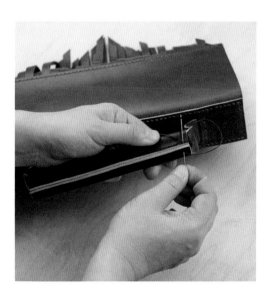

Weekender

Basic leathercraft kit (see p. 41)
Saddle stitching kit (see p. 41)

Materials
Vegetable-tanned leather, at least
    2 mm (5 oz) thickness (choose a
    softer leather for the body of the
    bag, but a less stretchy leather
    for the strap and shoulder pad)
Edge paint
Leather glue
Superglue
4 bag feet studs for the base
    (size of your choice)
60-cm (23½-in) zip
2 × 3.8-cm (1 ½-in) D-rings
2 × 3.8-cm (1 ½-in) swivel hooks
    or rings with opening
4 Sam Browne studs
    (medium-size bulb)
3–5-mm (⅛–¼-in) thick
    foam (optional)

Tools
Silver pen
Strap cutter
Paring knife
Granite/marble block
3-mm (⅛-in) hole punch
Palm hammer
Leather-palm glove (optional)
Bulldog clip (optional)
Plastic paddle
Roller

Techniques
Basic techniques (see p. 41)
Skiving (see p. 26)
Edge painting (see p. 34)
Burnishing straps (optional, see p. 34)
Gluing (see p. 28)
Saddle stitching (see p. 29)
Attaching a Sam Browne stud (see p. 37)

This design is a perfect weekend getaway bag.

It is designed to be carried across the shoulder with the adjustable strap or just with the handle, and has two handy side pockets for easy access to smaller items. The gussets on this bag are not dissimilar to the Toiletry Bag (see p. 94), but for this design they are pentagonal.

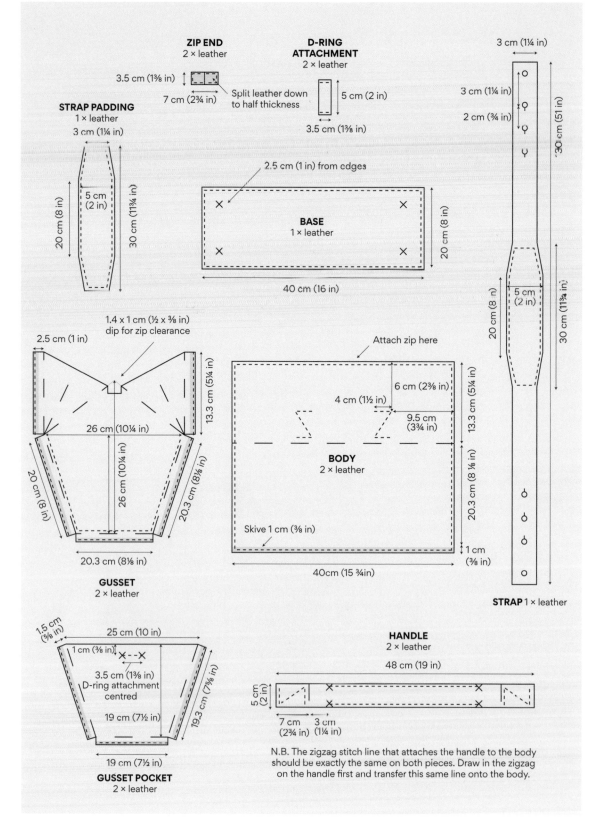

ZIP END
2 × leather

3.5 cm (1⅜ in)

7 cm (2¾ in)

Split leather down to half thickness

D-RING ATTACHMENT
2 × leather

5 cm (2 in)

3.5 cm (1⅜ in)

3 cm (1¼ in)

3 cm (1¼ in)

2 cm (¾ in)

30 cm (51 in)

STRAP PADDING
1 × leather

3 cm (1¼ in)

5 cm (2 in)

20 cm (8 in)

30 cm (11¾ in)

2.5 cm (1 in) from edges

BASE
1 × leather

20 cm (8 in)

40 cm (16 in)

20 cm (8 in)

5 cm (2 in)

30 cm (11¾ in)

STRAP 1 × leather

1.4 × 1 cm (½ × ⅜ in) dip for zip clearance

2.5 cm (1 in)

13.3 cm (5¼ in)

26 cm (10¼ in)

26 cm (10¼ in)

20 cm (8 in)

20.3 cm (8⅛ in)

20.3 cm (8⅛ in)

GUSSET
2 × leather

Attach zip here

6 cm (2⅜ in)

4 cm (1½ in)

9.5 cm (3¾ in)

13.3 cm (5¼ in)

BODY
2 × leather

20.3 cm (8⅛ in)

Skive 1 cm (⅜ in)

1 cm (⅜ in)

40cm (15 ¾in)

1.5 cm (⅝ in)

25 cm (10 in)

1 cm (⅜ in)

3.5 cm (1⅜ in) D-ring attachment centred

19 cm (7½ in)

19.3 cm (7⅝ in)

19 cm (7½ in)

GUSSET POCKET
2 × leather

HANDLE
2 × leather

48 cm (19 in)

5 cm (2 in)

7 cm (2¾ in)

3 cm (1¼ in)

N.B. The zigzag stitch line that attaches the handle to the body should be exactly the same on both pieces. Draw in the zigzag on the handle first and transfer this same line onto the body.

Method

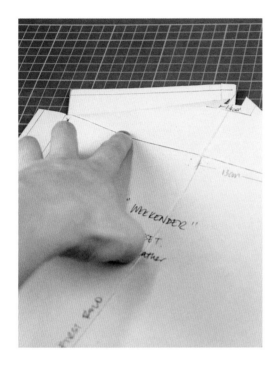

1. Prepare the pattern pieces

For the gusset, begin by getting your cut edge base perpendicular to your first fold. Measure and draw in the sides of the gusset by starting your measurements from this bottom cut edge and making use of the perpendicular first fold. Once drawn, add in the 2.5-cm (1-in) edge seam allowances. Cut out the gusset. Once cut, measure the sides of the gusset to get the exact measurements for the body piece. From the diagram, you can see that the side length of the bottom half of the gusset is the same as the length from the bottom of the body to the fold, and the side on the top half of the gusset is the same as the side of the top half of the body.

Use the same method of pattern making to make the gusset pocket. Create and cut out the other pattern pieces and add in all the prick marks, stitch lines and holes.

2. Cut the leather and hammer the stitch holes

Cut out the leather and transfer the markings. Use the softer leather for all pieces except for the strap and handle. I have used a contrasting black leather for the gusset pockets. Cut the handle with the strap cutter. Mark the position of the handle on the body and the placement of the gusset pockets on the gusset with an awl and score in the stitch lines with the awl and metal ruler. Skive down the edges as indicated and split the zip ends (see step 1 in the Toiletry Bag project on page 96). Score all the other stitch lines with the divider and hammer the stitch holes with the pricking chisel. All stitch holes should be made from the grain side, apart from the position of the gusset pocket on the gusset piece. Make the stitch holes for this from the back. Punch the holes on the strap and base using a 3-mm (⅛-in) hole punch. Make the keyholes for the Sam Browne studs on the strap.

3. Edge paint

Sand down all the edges with sandpaper. Then edge paint the top edges of the gusset and the body pieces. Edge paint the top and bottom edge of the base and all the sides of the gusset pocket and handle, as well as the strap. You may choose to burnish the strap instead by using a leather-palm glove.

- - - - - - - -

4. Attach the handles to the body

Create a rounded handle by stitching the handle lengthwise. To do this, use a plastic paddle to apply leather glue to the back of the stitch line on the long sides between the prick marks. Glue the sides together while matching the stitch holes. Saddle stitch along this stitch line. Once completed, you can sand it down slightly and reapply edge paint to create a more refined finish. Repeat for the other handle.

Apply leather glue to the ends of one handle and place them on the body as indicated to stick them down. Saddle stitch the handle to the body. Repeat on the other side.

- - - - - - - -

5. Attach the body to the base

Attach the feet to the base before assembling the pieces. On the back of the base, slot the screw thread of the feet into the 3-mm (⅛-in) hole. Apply a small amount of superglue to the tip of the screw thread and screw on the feet on the grain side. Repeat for the other feet. To attach the base to the body, place one piece of the body grain side up, with the bottom stitch line closest to you. Then place the base grain side up over the top of the body, matching its top stitch line to the bottom stitch line of the body. Apply leather glue or use a bulldog clip to secure one end, then saddle stitch the pieces together. Repeat on the other side.

6. Attach the zip to the body

Prepare the zip by attaching the zip ends. Follow the steps 5 and 6 on pages 97 and 98 in the Toiletry Bag project (omit the magnets). Before attaching the zip to the body, measure the zip to ensure that there will be equal lengths on either side once it is glued down. The zip is longer than the bag and there should be 10 cm (4 in) of zip on either side. Apply leather glue to the top stitch edge of the body and glue down the zip. Saddle stitch the zip to the body of the bag.

----

7. Attach the D-rings and gusset pockets to the gusset

Apply leather glue to the stitch line on the D-ring attachment, and on the grain and back side of the position of the D-ring on the gusset pocket. Once the glue is tacky, pull the D-ring attachment through the D-ring and wrap the D-ring attachment around the top edge of the gusset pocket, taking care to align the stitch holes. Saddle stitch this together before moving on to the next pocket.

Use a palm hammer to reinforce the folds on the gusset pocket. Then lay the gusset pocket over the gusset, matching the stitch holes. Saddle stitch these pieces together. Before moving on to the next step, reinforce the fold lines of the gusset using a roller, or hammer down gently with a palm hammer.

8. Attach the gusset to the body

To assemble the bag, apply a thin layer of glue to the back of the stitch edges of the gusset and on the stitch edges of the body and base sides. Once the glue is tacky, glue down the corners of the gusset in the correct position before manipulating the rest into place, so that no excess leather suddenly appears where the top of the gusset meets the top of the body at the zip. Glue the opposite side as well before saddle stitching to complete the bag.

- - - - - - - -

9. Final edge paint and assemble
the shoulder strap

Once the stitching is complete, sand down the edges to get rid of any glue and loose fibres and apply edge paint.

Stitch the padded area of the shoulder strap by aligning the strap padding to the centre of the strap. Apply a thin layer of glue to the back of the stitch line and glue in place. Saddle stitch this together to form a padded area for the shoulder. Before attaching these pieces, you may wish to add a piece of foam (slightly smaller on all sides than the "strap padding") in between to give it extra padding.

Once completed, slot the ends of the strap through the swivel hooks. Attach the Sam Browne studs with the bulb tops on the back of the leather. Secure the strap by pushing the Sam Browne studs into the keyholes.

- - - - - - - -

Suppliers

UK

J. T. Batchelor
9–10 Culford Mews, London N1 4DZ
+44 (0)20 7254 2962

Walter Reginald
Unit 6, 100 The Highway, London E1W 2BX
+44 (0)20 7481 2233
www.walterreginald.co.uk

Alma Leather
Block D, 12–14 Greatorex St, London E1 5NF
+44 (0)20 7377 0762
www.almaleather.co.uk

Leprevo
1 Charlotte Square, Newcastle upon Tyne NE1 4XF
+44 (0)191 232 4179
www.leprevo.co.uk

Metropolitan Leather
10 Cottingham Way, Thrapston, Kettering NN14 4PL
+44 (0)1832 732216
www.metropolitanleather.com

A & A Crack
16 Pennard Close, Northampton NN4 7BE
+44 (0)1604 874422
www.aacrack.co.uk

Pittards
Sherborne Road, Yeovil, Somerset BA21 5BA
+44 (0)1935 474321
www.pittards.com

S & K Camden
10 Pratt Mews, London NW1 0AD
+44 (0)20 7354 4435
www.skfittings.co.uk

London Trimmings
28 Cambridge Heath Road, Whitechapel, London E1 5QH
+44 (0)207 790 2233
www.londontrimmings.co.uk

Europe

Gruppo Mastrotto
Zona Industriale, Quarta Strada 7,
36071 Arzignano (Vi), Italy
+39 0444 621200
www.mastrotto.com

The Genuine Italian Vegetable-Tanned Leather Consortium
Via Primo Maggio 82/84,
Ponte a Egola 56028 San Miniato - Pisa – Italy
+39 0571 485158
www.pellealvegetale.it

Senatori
Via di Casellina, 42 50018 Scandicci, Firenze, Italy
www.senatorispa.it

ABC Morini
Via Ilio Barontini, 15/b, S.Colombano 50018,
Scandicci, Firenze, Italy
+39 055 722571
www.abcmorini.net

Echtleer
Oester 30–32, 1723 HW Noord-Scharwoude, Netherlands
+31 6 15062177
www.echtleer.nl

USA

Tandy Leather
1900 SE Loop 820 Bldg B, Fort Worth, TX 76140
+1 1 877 532 8437
www.tandyleather.com

Weaver Leather
7540 CR 201, PO Box 68, Mount Hope, OH 44660
+1 330 674 1782
www.weaverleather.com

United Leather
1414 Newton Street, Los Angeles, CA 90021
+1 213 747 1723
www.unitedleather.com

Springfield Leather
1463 S. Glenstone Ave, Springfield, MO 65804
+1 1 800 668 8518
www.springfieldleather.com

Index

About the Author

Candice Lau is an award-winning leatherworker based in London. She designs stylish bags and accessories inspired by modern, functional living. She is passionate about using and promoting traditional leathercraft methods and runs regular workshops from her London studio.

Acknowledgements

The deepest and most special thanks to my daughter, Matilde, for inspiring and motivating me to work incredibly hard to get the book written before her arrival into the world. To my husband, Mattia, for his dedication and talent in working on the photography for the book. Finally, to my family for their support and especially to my beautiful grandmother for teaching me to be the person I am today. Huge thanks to the team at Octopus who have worked so hard to guide me through this experience and helped me to create this book.
